LEADERSHIP TWO WORDS AT A TIME

Other Works by Bill Treasurer

Right Risk
10 Powerful Principles for Taking Giant Leaps with Your Life

Positively M.A.D.
Making A Difference in Your Organizations, Communities, and the World

Courage Goes to Work
How to Build Backbones, Boost Performance, and Get Results

Leaders Open Doors
A Radically Simple Leadership Approach to Lift People, Profits, and Performance
(ATD Press, 978-1-5628-6857-4)

A Leadership Kick in the Ass
How to Learn from Rough Landings, Blunders, and Missteps

The Leadership Killer
Reclaiming Humility in an Age of Arrogance
Coauthored with Capt. John Havlik, Retired Navy SEAL
(Little Leaps Press, Inc.)

LEADERSHIP TWO WORDS AT A TIME

SIMPLE TRUTHS FOR LEADING COMPLICATED PEOPLE

BILL TREASURER

Berrett–Koehler Publishers, Inc.

Berrett-Koehler Publishers, Inc.
1333 Broadway, Suite 1000
Oakland, CA 94612-1921
Tel: (510) 817-2277
Fax: (510) 817-2278
www.bkconnection.com

ORDERING INFORMATION

Quantity sales. Special discounts are available on quantity purchases by corporations, associations, and others. For details, contact the "Special Sales Department" at the Berrett-Koehler address above.

Individual sales. Berrett-Koehler publications are available through most bookstores. They can also be ordered directly from Berrett-Koehler: Tel: (800) 929-2929; Fax: (802) 864-7626; www.bkconnection.com.

Orders for college textbook / course adoption use. Please contact Berrett-Koehler: Tel: (800) 929-2929; Fax: (802) 864-7626.

Distributed to the U.S. trade and internationally by Penguin Random House Publisher Services.

Printed in Canada

Berrett-Koehler books are printed on long-lasting acid-free paper. When it is available, we choose paper that has been manufactured by environmentally responsible processes. These may include using trees grown in sustainable forests, incorporating recycled paper, minimizing chlorine in bleaching, or recycling the energy produced at the paper mill.

Library of Congress Cataloging-in-Publication Data
Names: Treasurer, Bill, 1962- author.
Title: Leadership two words at a time : simple truths for leading complicated people / Bill Treasurer.
Description: First Edition. | Oakland, CA : Berrett-Koehler Publishers, [2022] | Includes bibliographical references and index.
Identifiers: LCCN 2022011315 (print) | LCCN 2022011316 (ebook) | ISBN 9781523003174 (paperback) | ISBN 9781523003181 (pdf) | ISBN 9781523003198 (epub) | ISBN 9781523003204
Subjects: LCSH: Leadership. | Leadership—Psychological aspects. | Trust.
Classification: LCC HD57.7 .T7354 2022 (print) | LCC HD57.7 (ebook) | DDC 658.4/092—dc23/eng/20220506
LC record available at https://lccn.loc.gov/2022011315
LC ebook record available at https://lccn.loc.gov/2022011316

First Edition
28 27 26 25 24 23 22 10 9 8 7 6 5 4 3 2 1

Book producer and text designer: Detta Penna
Copyeditor: Susan Schmid, Teton Editorial; Proofeader: Lerena Hebert, Sharp Eye
Cover designer: The Book Designers

TO THE NEXT GENERATION OF LEADERS,

TO WHOM OUR FUTURE IS ENTRUSTED:

BE COURAGEOUS

CONTENTS

WITTY AND WISE

Every once in a while, a book is written that speaks to your heart, mind, and soul. *Two Words* is one of those books. As I read the introduction for the first time, I kept thinking, "Is Bill a mind reader? How does he know this about me?" Then I realized that he knows what I need AND he knows how to present it so that I'll resonate with it.

WHY?

Why *Two Words*? Why this book? Bill claims that all the essential lessons he's learned about leadership can be summed up in two words—and then he goes about proving it. I've known Bill for a number of years. He is a self-proclaimed New Yorker, and he is not a man of few words. So, when he boils down all that he knows about leadership in two-word phrases I take notice!

Why should you read this book? Well, to use the two-word theme: What & How. What is in this book? How is the content presented?

WHAT?

What does *Two Words* offer that other books don't? There is no shortage of leadership books, but many books drone on and on filling lots of space with many words. Few books offer practical, implementable wisdom. And fewer still offer advice for the new leader. *Two Words* does both. Bill has taken all the dry, theoretical leadership content and turned it into practical and wise two-word directives that new leaders can implement immediately.

You will find advice from Bill and other leaders he's worked with. Of course, each chapter is titled with two words such as "Practice Humility," "Nurture Talent," and "Promote Inclusion." The advice within each chapter follows the same two-word theme. At the end of each chapter, Bill makes recommendations to ensure you take action to reach your next level of leadership. He provides two-word guidance for what you can Think Now and how you can Act Now. He even adds bonus tips such as SWOT Stuff and Provide Cover.

Of course, the content covers more than two-word gems. Although written for new leaders, we all know seasoned leaders who could use a couple of these to shore up their leadership skills:

- "Being your best self requires having a core set of principles that you live by."
- "Heads and hearts aren't supposed to be disconnected from each other."
- "As a leader, you must care deeply about the quality of your work."
- "Drawing out the best in others starts by reflecting the best of yourself."
- "No one wants to be led by a perfectly [alert: word-play action here] fake leader."

Bill delivers content that gives you something to think about whether you are a new or an experienced leader.

HOW?

How does *Two Words* present its wisdom? "How you say it matters as much as what you say," is a direct quote from *Two Words*. And Bill follows his own advice. He shares profoundly personal stories, hiding nothing. This is important because we often learn more from our mistakes than from our successes. He also uses examples from real life and introduces us to many respected leaders.

The book's wisdom is presented in professional down-to-earth reflections about topics. For example, while discussing trust, Bill asks you to consider how life has impacted your ability to trust, as well as how vulnerability is critical to being trusted.

Bill uses two-word phrases throughout that represent verbs or actions you can take as well as nouns or results you should achieve. Some of my favorite verbs/actions include Provide Cover, Create Opportunity, Persist Intentionally, Add Value, and Model Vulnerability. My favorite nouns/results include Purposeful Humility, Modern Modesty, and No Surprises. Now I ask you—how many more words do you need to enact these leadership requirements?

Bill uses unpretentious language to make his points. For example, when sharing his feelings of once-a-year performance reviews, he describes them as, "a septic tank ready to explode all over the employee." And he is brutally honest with readers, telling us: "don't brown-nose" and "don't be chintzy." If that isn't enough, he punctuates his advice with words such as, "ouch," "tough noogies," and "urp!" Yep, you know he's talking directly to you! Feeling deflated about your leadership skills? Bill would say, "Fuggedabout it!" You can feel Bill's vibrant personality come through on every page, as if he is standing next to you.

But, should you worry there isn't enough depth for you, fret not. The writing goes way beyond using witty, hard-hitting earthy humor as Bill draws on Rodin's statues, Dante's Inferno, and the Sword of Damocles to make powerful points. Yes, there is enough depth for any leader, new or experienced.

Bottom line? Bill says a lot in two words, and he probably could have boiled this book down to less than two-hundred two-word phrases printed in a book about eight pages long. How's that for economical writing? But then we would have lost the poignant stories, his New York attitude, and all of his witty words. Bill uses a refreshing style to deliver practical wisdom to leaders at all career stages. The book is both witty and wise.

Every once in a while, a book comes along that you don't want to end. *Two Words* is one of those books. But end it must—because you can't just read about leadership. You need to—two words and a drum roll, please:

PRACTICE LEADERSHIP

Elaine Biech, author
Skills for Career Success

YOU MATTER

Something important is about to happen, and I know you can feel it. You, the one who has learned to believe in yourself, trust yourself, and follow the quiet inner voice that says, "Why not me?" You don't think you're "better" than other people; you've just learned through ups and downs, the gruel and the grind, and ordeals and adventures that you can find a way to overcome obstacles and finish the landing. And when you do, you make improvements so you can land closer to perfect next time. There is always more to do and better ways to do it.

You're an achiever, someone blessed with divine discontent. You're never fully satisfied with where you are because you know that with creativity, ingenuity, and effort, any "great job" of today can be outdone tomorrow. Yes, you like to compete, and yes, you like to win. But winning is so much sweeter when you beat your own best, competing against yourself, and topping your last big achievement. You want others to top themselves too. You expect more, of yourself and others.

You're impatient, yes, but in a way that brings urgency to the task at hand, not in a way that adds to the risk or jeopardizes progress. You're impatient because you're passionate; you know that the pursuit of the outcomes will lift everyone's skills and deepen their experience. Progress demands momentum, and momentum turns on the engine of urgency.

You keep your foot on the throttle because it moves things forward. You give a rip.

You're a learner, a seeker, a curious venturer. You're alert, interested, and engaged, and when you aren't, you scan the landscape for something new to reenergize your brain cells. Your learning is perpetual because you're never done. You want answers that are more precise, accurate, truthful, and enduring. You study, review, and challenge, knowing skepticism is part of the calculation and thoughtfulness that lead to decisions and actions that are safer, sounder, and more likely to succeed.

You pay attention to others who have traveled further down the road, accomplished grander things, or overcome bigger obstacles. You go out of your way to learn about the experiences and stories of those who are commonly ignored, dismissed, or excluded. You are humble enough to listen to everyone, and smart enough to heed advice coming from anyone. You aim to use whatever advantages you have enjoyed to make the workplace more fair, just, and equitable for everyone. You use your voice to amplify the concerns of those whose voices are too often suppressed. You treat no one as lesser. Ever.

You haven't had it easy. You've experienced setbacks, barriers, and people who weren't on your side. Despite that, or because of it, you strive to see and expect the best in others—even those who withhold those courtesies from you. You're a believer in human potential. As much as you believe in your own abilities, you know that your game is upped by people who play an upped game, so you take the time to teach, coach, and serve others. You have little interest in going it alone, as your goals and aspirations are bigger than you could achieve all on your own. Besides, working with fiercely independent individuals who choose to put the team's interests above their own is more fun than flying solo.

Some of you can calculate numbers in your head. Some of you have always been "good with people." Some of you have a knack for pinpointing risks. Some of you have spatial awareness and can conceptualize what finished rooms or buildings will look like before they are built. Some of you excel at forecasting scenarios and setting the master plan. Though the talents may be different, all of you have proven yourself to yourself. Many times over, whether in school, on the sports field, or in how responsibly you've performed your first jobs, you've shown up and gotten the job done. You and I know you're going to have to prove yourself to many others in the future—and you're up to that challenge. In fact, you relish it.

Others see you on the cusp of becoming a leader. But you and I know differently. You already are a leader. And you're just getting started.

YOUR POTENTIAL

I've seen where you could end up. Over time, people like you take on greater responsibility and pursue grander challenges. They are granted more decision authority, brought in on more consequential situations, and entrusted with bigger teams and budgets. They are given more latitude over who gets hired or fired. They come to add more value to the organization than they are compensated for, improving operations, processes, people, and profits. They leave the people and organization far better off than they found them.

I've watched people like you yearn to make a bigger difference. I've witnessed them stumble, be hard on themselves, and then figure out how to move forward. I've seen them grapple with how to confront situations...or people.

I've thought with them, strategized with them, laughed with them, and, because I fully believed in them, firmly challenged them. Most of all, I've learned from them. What they've taught me is what I will share with you so that you too can reach your full leadership potential.

I've seen people like you before they moved into their first leadership role, as they labored, developed, and excelled in the role, and eventually transitioned out of it. I've seen people like you progress from self-performer, to leading a small team, to leading a big team, to leading multiple teams, to leading divisions, to competently running entire business units worth over a billion dollars. And I've seen people like you positively impact the careers of hundreds of others, many of whom went on to become leaders in their own right.

This could be you. You could get there too. Down deep, I know you know that. "Why not me?" right?

MY BACKSTORY

As a practitioner of leadership development, I believe in the power of leadership to transform lives. I believe that because my own life has been transformed by the leaders who shaped me since the start of my career. I'll soon share a condensed version of my backstory in the hopes that it will inspire you to trace your own. What strikes me about the leaders who led me is how they continue to apply their influence today, even in the late stages of their careers or lives. That says something about the enduring nature of leadership as a constructive force for good. A leader's primary job—to bring about positive change—is never fully done.

My first "real" job was as a junior consultant at High Performing Systems, where I worked under the guidance of a retired U.S. Army Special Forces officer, Dr. Henry L. Thompson, who had done two tours in Vietnam in covert operations. He was, and is, a leader in every sense of the word (now in his seventies, he still competes in Ironman® races, dedicating his runs to fallen heroes). Later, I led over 300 outdoor team building events as vice president of program services for Executive Adventure. My boss, Bob Carr, was a pioneer in outdoor experiential education. Today, along with his wife Anne, Bob runs Common Courtesy, Inc., an organization that arranges free transportation for elderly adults. Later still, I joined Accenture, one of the world's largest management and technology consulting firms. I was in the firm's change management and human performance practice, and worked with Hines Brannan, who was a managing partner of Accenture. Now "retired," he serves on multiple boards and is currently the board chairman of the Mississippi State University Foundation where he was recently awarded an honorary doctoral degree for his leadership and public service. Eventually, with Hines's encouragement and support, I became Accenture's first full time internal executive coach, regularly coaching some thirty-five leaders...all of whom outranked me.

Leadership is a confidence– and capability-building profession. Meaning that, ideally, leaders leave us more confident and capable than they found us. Guided by their influence, we gain more skills and expertise so we can add more value for those we serve. The more value we add, the more substantial our positive contributions become. Getting to that point requires our leaders to draw out our latent skills, provide candid or course-correcting feedback, nudge us outside of our comfort zones so we take on hard tasks, and hold us to higher standards than we sometimes prefer to hold ourselves. The yield on all this deliberate leadership guidance should be a better and more capable us, so that we can have a similar positive impact on those we influence through our leadership. Good leaders beget good leaders. How has this worked in your life? Who are the leaders who shaped you, and how are you better off as a result? More importantly, how are you carrying to others the benefits that you gained from those who led you?

US, TOGETHER

Some twenty years ago, drawing on the lessons of the leaders who impacted me, I founded my own consulting firm, Giant Leap Consulting. Today I regularly work with leaders like you, or the leaders you have the potential to become. I design, develop, and deliver leadership programs for emerging and experienced leaders alike. Through the work of my company, I've been fortunate to have worked with literally thousands of leaders in the United States and beyond. I learned far more about leadership from the leaders with whom I've worked than I ever did in graduate school...where I studied leadership. I took what all those leaders taught me and wove it into the leadership programs I've produced and the leadership books I've written.

While I've worked with leaders of all levels of experience, my favorite leaders, and those with whom I've worked the most, are new leaders. I learn a lot from them. There's a certain energy and eagerness that makes working with new leaders like you so enjoyable. New leaders' self-doubt, receptivity, and coachability are much higher, making whatever contributions I can make to their advancement feel that much more rewarding.

I've wanted to write this book for a long, long time. But as an author, I've learned that you write what you can write at the time when you can write it. I couldn't have written

Leadership Two Words at a Time thirty years ago, at least not credibly. I had to earn the right to write this book. It took thousands of one-on-one executive coaching conversations and thousands of hours working closely with developing leaders to gain the knowledge, practical guidance, and, frankly, confidence to have gotten to this point.

My work has been done in partnership with leaders as they've led. Like a field anthropologist living among a tribe of chieftains, I dwell with the leaders whom others study from a distance. I'm grateful to be an insider/outsider, an accepted member of the tribe yet with enough distance to draw independent observations. Many of the leaders who have taught me, lead teams that produce real, tangible, and concrete outcomes—such as bridges, highways, commercial buildings, and data centers. The consequences of failure are not hypothetical—they are catastrophic. Some of the leaders helm multi-billion-dollar companies, others lead the field crews that build the jobs from which those companies derive their revenue. The lessons to come are drawn from the nitty-gritty leadership trenches, where real leaders toil to get things right, the answers aren't always clear-cut, and ambiguities abound. In a very real way, this book was coauthored by thousands of struggling leaders...just like you.

YOUR INVITATION

You'll get more out of this book if you trust me. For some of you, I'll earn that trust as the chapters unfold and you start to draw value from what's shared. For more disarmed folks, that trust may come earlier. Regardless, please know that I'm not out to manipulate or harm you. You've been given a wonderful opportunity to lead others, and my aim is to help you do great things with it. The stories, insights, tips, and essential lessons are focused on helping you have a thriving leadership career so you can make a true and positive difference in the lives you'll impact through your leadership.

In the spirit of full disclosure, please recognize that despite the positive impact that leaders, young and old, have had on me, I can be judgy, irritable, self-righteous, opinionated, pushy, and glib. Sometimes that human material may leak onto the pages. My aim isn't to be off-putting, just real. I'm guessing you'd rather read the words of an imperfect author who's striving to be better, than a pious one who presumes their eventual sainthood.

I believe in you and your potential, and I want your leadership experience to be satisfying and successful. I invite you to think of me as your own personal coach as you progress through the chapters. I aim to have the same positive impact on you that the leaders with whom I've worked and coached have had on me and many others. I'm going to tell it to you straight, not with a finger pointed in your face admonishing your shortfalls, but with an eye toward the better person we both know you can become. I promise not to patronize you or treat you with kid gloves. Think of me as the person you can count on to privately motion you that you've got broccoli in your teeth at the lunch meeting. Here and there I'll hold up the mirror so that you can see yourself clearly, but always with the intention of increasing your self-awareness and promoting the better leader we both want you to become. You matter, and, as a new leader, you are at a critical point in your leadership journey. The habits, practices, and mindset you adopt now will stay with you throughout your career. Today you're a new leader. My focus in writing this book is on the strong and seasoned leader you're capable of becoming. Yes, something important is about to happen. This book will help you be ready for it.

INTRODUCTION

THE PLIGHT OF NEW LEADERS

Congratulations, new leader, you've joined the leadership ranks at an exceptionally complicated time. The world in which you will operate is fraught with touchy political divisions, economic disparities, generational tensions, and racial disharmonies. Magnifying the difficulty are the ever-shifting dynamics of today's workplace. More leaders are leading remote teams across larger geographic distances, presenting unique challenges in terms of onboarding new employees, giving performance feedback, building esprit de corps, and nurturing healthy relationships. The traditional stability of consistently applied standard operating work protocols has also been upended. Now individual exceptions and customized deals are common, tailored to flexibly accommodate each person's extenuating life realities. Today's leaders struggle to treat everyone fairly, yet individually. Letting one person work from home three days a week to care for an immunocompromised parent may make sense to you, but it may not make sense to the healthy single person you require to be onsite every day. You'll simultaneously be seen as exceedingly fair or unfair, depending on who benefits from policy exceptions that today's realities require you to allow.

While the realities facing new leaders are unprecedently novel, challenging, and anxiety-provoking, the meager amount of support and training that has historically been provided to new leaders remains, sadly, unchanged. According to Development Dimensions Inc.'s Global Leadership Forecast, 83 percent of organizations say it's important to develop leaders, but only 5 percent have fully implemented plans to do so. While your organization may not be intentionally setting you up to fail, they likely aren't setting you up to succeed either.

If you're not getting the new-leader training you need, you're likely to seek out leadership guidance on your own—as well you should. Even if you do, though, you're likely to be disappointed. Most leadership books are targeted at experienced leaders whose leadership challenges and developmental needs are far different from those of new leaders like you. C-level executives (CEO, CFO, COO, etc.) and senior leaders (EVP, SVP, VP, etc.) are a tiny fraction of the overall leadership ranks, yet the bulk of leadership advice goes to them—the already-experienced. The more urgent and unique needs of first-time and mid-level leaders like you go largely unaddressed. Advising a C-level exec to "establish a clear organizational value proposition" is sound guidance. Giving the same advice to a new project manager who is frantically trying to keep her under-resourced team on task is a ridiculous waste of time. New leaders aren't trying to go from good to great, they're just trying to survive till the end of the week.

PILING ON

Transitioning into your first leadership role can be hugely challenging and most new leaders are wholly unprepared for it. Getting promoted into a leadership role is often your reward for delivering exceptional individual performance. A high-potential person gets noticed for working harder and

- Ego inflation is the most dangerous leadership ailment of all.
- The more you manage and tame your ego, the better the leader you will be.

Chapter 6 Cultivate Composure *How cultivating composure will help you manage your ego while keeping your motives and intentions pure*

- People don't want to be led by hotheads.
- Composure, level-headedness, and reasonableness are essential to effective leadership.
- How practicing centeredness ensures that you'll act in ways that are consistent with your deepest and purest values.
- Silence and meditation change your perspective on everything...for the better.

Part II, Leading People, deals with those demanding, fickle, and ever-changing resources: human beings. This section covers your role as nurturer, developer, and encourager of talent, and your direct responsibility to promote an inclusive environment that inspires people to give their very best.

Chapter 7 Trust First *Why trust is essential to developing strong relationships, with practical tips for building it*

- You will fail as a leader if you can't figure out how to trust those you're leading.
- The vibes you transmit to others will tell them whether they can trust you.
- Trust takes vulnerability, and vulnerability takes courage.

Chapter 8 Create Safety *Why creating psychological safety is your best way of ensuring that the people you're leading will have the courage to innovate and improve*

- Too many leaders still use fear to motivate people to get things done.
- The people you lead will be courageous when they know it's safe to do so.
- Your composure is key to creating a safe work environment.
- There are healthy and mature ways to confront direct reports.

Chapter 9 Nurture Talent *How spending focused time developing each individual who reports to you adds value to the organization and to their careers*

- Delegation does more than free up your time: it is a powerful means of developing the skills of your direct reports.
- Development takes a person-to-person time investment.
- Making people uncomfortable—in a good way—is part of your job.

Chapter 10 Promote Inclusion *What you can do to provide a welcoming, equitable, diverse, and inclusive environment for everyone you're privileged to lead*

- Everyone has biases. As a leader, you need to guard against allowing yours to favor certain people over others.
- There are a host of tangible benefits of a diverse workplace.
- As a leader, you should do more than just "accept" diversity...you should promote it.

Part III, Leading Work, focuses on the strategic and operational aspects of getting work done. The whole point of leadership is to produce positive outcomes that didn't exist before. Leaders do that by setting goals and priorities, employing sound management, promoting ownership and accountability, and getting work done.

Chapter 11 Love Business *Why business can initially be intimidating, and how you can, and must, learn to love it*

- Leadership requires knowing, understanding, and loving business.
- All organizations, even nonprofits and government agencies, involve business.
- Business can be a spirited adventure, inspiring your creativity and seasoning your judgment.

Chapter 12 Get Results *Why the whole point of leadership is to deliver results that are positive and sustainable, and what you can do to increase the likelihood that you will*

- As a leader, you'll be judged based on whether you can "make it happen."
- The pressure to get results will stay with you as long as you serve in a leadership role.
- The most satisfying results are those that take a long time to produce.
- Your bosses will expect that the results you delivered today will be exceeded tomorrow.

Chapter 13 Master Management *Why work needs to be more than led—it has to be managed...by doing these things*

- Good management starts with clear goals.
- To truly motivate, goals need to be explicit and aggressive.

- To promote shared accountability, you have to clarify expectations and inspect the work.
- "Acting like an owner" means being financially responsible!

Chapter 14 Lead Up *Why you have to carefully, thoughtfully, and deliberately lead one audience in particular: your bosses*

- Supporting your boss's success is your job.
- The more you get involved in extracurricular corporate activities, the stronger your network will be.
- The fastest way to get promoted is to think beyond your boss's thinking.

In the pages to come, you'll learn what it takes to be and stay a leader. You'll learn memorable two-word leadership essentials that you can put to good use right away. I've done my best to explain these essentials in a clear-cut way. For those who have read my other books, you know I'm big on using quotes from famous people. This time, nearly all the quotes are from real-life leaders like you. I hope you find them relatable and instructive.

AGELESSLY NEW

At some point on their leadership journey, most leaders reflect back and think, "I wish I had known then what I know now." This book is to help you know now what other leaders learn later in their careers. Thus, the book wasn't written to share newfangled methods with crusty old late-stage leaders. It's to share ageless and tested wisdom with folks just starting out on their leadership journey. My biased opinion is that the book has value for seasoned leaders too. Leadership is one of those topics that benefit from constant reminders, so even older leaders are bound to find something new. After all,

REMOTE REALITIES

"Wait! Hold on!" you might be thinking, "What about having to lead teams remotely? How am I supposed to lead people who are so far away from me?" I'm with you, and I understand your concern. We've all lived through the challenges of having to communicate, coordinate, and get work done while working from home. You're right: leading remotely presents genuine leadership challenges in terms of onboarding new employees, giving performance feedback, building esprit de corps, and nurturing healthy relationships. Beyond that, spending countless hours on computer meetings is plain exhausting. True enough! That said, this is not a book specifically devoted to remote leadership. Happily, the experience of the last few years has resulted in a glut of books, articles, podcasts, and other resources on that topic. Seriously, search for "remote leadership resources" at least fifty billion results (I just checked!). Regardless, you'll be glad to know that, with a little finessing, nearly every tip in this book can be applied with the people you're leading, whether you're physically present with them or not.

what other leadership book has a whole chapter dedicated to Cultivating Composure?!

TWO AGAIN

Over the years I've found that new leaders often make things much harder than they need to. They get in their own way a lot. They get mired in the weeds and take on too much themselves, becoming off-center and grumpy. They live in their heads a lot, overthinking and overplanning, and getting overwhelmed in the process. They rely too much on brown-nosing, and not enough on truth-telling and transparency. They get the alchemy between relationship and task wrong, either being likable to the point of being a pushover or dominant to the point where people want to mutiny. In extreme cases, they start to lose confidence in themselves, or worse, their direct reports and bosses start to lose confidence in them. The harder they make leadership, the less effective they are and the less enjoyable it becomes. To date, very few books, if any, have addressed the unique plight of new leaders, much less offered essential leadership guidance to help them thrive in their new leadership roles.

As noted, thirty years working with new leaders have convinced me that nearly all the most important truths about leadership can be boiled down into simple two-word concepts. What do I mean? Let me share one of the first two-word leadership lessons I learned during my years at Accenture. There was a partner named Larry Coates who was sort of a mix between Bill Gates and Emmett Lathrop "Doc" Brown, PhD, the wild-eyed inventor played perfectly by Christopher Lloyd in the Back to the Future movies. Larry had a brilliant technical mind and served as the technical lead for hundreds of project teams. (He was also a skilled barefoot water-skier!) The two-word leadership imperative that Larry would often share with new consultants was memorable, useful, and critically important: No Surprises!

It took very little explaining for Larry to relay the two-word concept: bring people in to help you solve problems before they become bigger problems and explode in your face. This simple yet wise leadership advice has been shared by thousands of seasoned leaders to their less-experienced counterparts throughout the ages. It's a lesson involving discipline, courage, and risk mitigation, all of which we'll explore when we revisit this two-word lesson more fully later in the book.

While this book may be the first to be built around two-word leadership essentials, the business world is full of other important concepts and functions that are described with two-word titles. A tiny sample includes emotional intelligence, psychological safety, employee engagement, talent management, operational excellence, continuous improvement, business development, customer service, strategic planning, and servant leadership.

PLEASE ENGAGE!

Novelist Courtney C. Stevens, author of *The Lies About Truth*, says, "If nothing changes, nothing changes." That certainly applies to leadership development.

To support you in committing to positive leadership changes that you identify as you read the book, at the end of each part, you'll be asked to sign an oath. Leaders keep promises, and the three oaths you'll sign will be to yourself, to the people you'll lead, and to the work you'll do. Throughout the book, you'll also be encouraged to sharpen your leadership point of view by answering leadership-related questions that appear at the end of each chapter under the header Think Now. But thinking is not enough—you can't think yourself into behavioral change. Only action will do that. Thus, each chapter also concludes with specific and immediate actions you can take to apply what you've learned, under the header Act Now. The aim of the book is to be memorable, practical, and useful. So, as you engage with it, you'll actively do what leaders do: envision outcomes, make commitments, and take action! (Notice the two words?) Are you ready to go to work? Good. Start with the questions and actions below.

THINK NOW/*ACT NOW*

Think Now

What attracts you to leadership?

Why do you think you're fit to lead?

At the end of your career, what impact do you hope to make through your leadership?

What do you hope to learn by reading this book that will strengthen your leadership impact? Where do you feel you could use more confidence?

Act Now

- List the names of people who you know that you consider to be leaders.
- Pick one of those leaders and reach out to them to have a conversation about leadership.
- Start documenting your own Leadership Lessons using whatever note-taking tool is most convenient for you.

PART I

LEADING YOURSELF

You leading you. That's what this first section is devoted to. Leading yourself is the starting point for learning how to lead others. All the essentials involved in leading others, such as having a vision, understanding motivation, developing skills, trust and empowerment, and corrective action, apply to leading yourself as well. Not to be harsh, but if you can't lead yourself, what qualifies you to lead others? You won't have much credibility leading others if you can't lead yourself out of a paper bag.

Leading yourself is an aspect of your leadership that can become increasingly strained as the responsibilities and burdens of leadership grow in significance. Other people, situations, and obligations can slowly creep up your priority list, while you keep slinking down on it. Self-neglect is a real danger for leadership careerists, sabotaging their well-being, health, and leadership fitness. Thus, learning to lead yourself, with fidelity and consistency, will serve you well and bring sanity to your leadership of others.

CHAPTER 1

KNOW THYSELF

Transform Your Leadership with Self-Awareness

The starting point of leadership is self-knowledge. You've got to be intimately familiar with your inner workings. You've got to know what makes you tick, and what ticks you off. You've got to know your values, interests, talents, and triggers. You've got to be clear about what you can do well, and what you'd do well to have others do. You've got to know what energizes and de-energizes you, and what you're drawn to and repelled by. You've got to know which time of day your creative juices flow, and when you're prone to making mistakes. You've also got to be clear about the challenges you've dealt with or overcome and how they shaped you, and honest about whatever unearned advantages and privileges you may have benefitted from, so you have compassion for the disadvantaged. You've got to know you. Really well.

Having run a courage-building consulting company for two decades, I'm now convinced that the single greatest courageous action any human being can take is the journey to the center of one's self. This journey of self-discovery takes bravely facing and accepting various truths about yourself. It means coming to terms with all facets of your very human nature, good and bad.

Each person, including every leader, is a pair of opposites. Knowing Thyself will teach you that you are likely caring, passionate, smart, disciplined, generous, and good. You are also likely occasionally judgy, uptight, petty, selfish, and less-than-good. In other words, you're human! Just like every other leader who has ever lived.

Depending on the situation, mood, or even sheer randomness, you may be happy or glum, content or anxious, trusting or suspicious, confident or unsure, generous or piggish. None of those characteristics needs to be rooted out. There's no need to reject the "bad" elements of yourself because what constitutes "bad" is always shifting. All your emotions can be appropriate or inappropriate depending on the context. There are plenty of work instances where impatience, skepticism, hesitancy, and even fright or anger is the right emotional response and plenty where such emotions will do damage.

One's thoughts precede and, more importantly, dictate one's actions. Knowing what's going on in your inner world and being able to gently tame your thoughts and emotions will keep wild mood swings from impacting your outer world. A lot of wreckage has been left in the wake of leaders who let their emotions get the best of them. Left uncontrolled, anger, resentment, jealousy and envy, revenge, and lust are potent poisons, and nearly always result in failed leadership. That doesn't mean you have to be emotionally neutered—you are human after all—but it does mean you have to be mindful of the effects your inner self is having on the people you outwardly lead. Be attuned to the fact that your personhood will have a direct impact on their reactions and results. The ability to observe our own thoughts and feelings and alter them when they are undermining us is what differentiates us from wild beasts.

As a new leader, you have one key self-reflective question you should ask yourself anytime you feel angry, frustrated, anxious, or emotionally charged: What fear might be behind this? Very often, the reason you're so upset is that you're fearful you will lose something, or not get something you feel you deserve. As a leader, you will learn that your fear, wherever it comes from, will be your biggest enemy and inhibitor. Nothing will twist your actions, decisions, and attitude as much as being afraid that you're not going to get the [fill-in-the-blank: recognition, compensation, acknowledgement, admiration, respect] that you think you deserve. The journey to the center of yourself takes courage because it involves confronting your fears.

The value of the journey of self-discovery is that it helps you take a personal inventory of everything that makes you you. Knowing yourself will also help you better understand those around you. While your values, thoughts, and emotions are uniquely your own, they are also universally felt. They will help you relate to the people you're leading. As you advance as a leader, in influence, power, and stature, people will want to know that at the core human level you haven't forgotten that you are just like them. They need to know that when they are upset, overwhelmed, or feeling insecure, you know where they're coming from because you know what it's like to feel those feelings. They understand that you may operate at a higher rung on the organizational ladder, but they want to know that you get where they are coming from, that you are made of the same gooey human source material, and that you have had, and can relate to, their hopes and hurts.

As a leader, you will learn that your fear, wherever it comes from, will be your biggest enemy and inhibitor.

When you're in a leadership role, it's vital to have a clear understanding of human nature. You will spend the bulk of your time dealing with human beings and all their fickle insecurities and eccentricities. Self-awareness is a key differentiator between successful and unsuccessful leaders. People's insides always affect their outsides. Knowing how people's emotions impact their morale, well-being, and performance is a first-order responsibility. After taking personal inventory of your own emotional disposition and understanding how your emotions impact others, you will be much less perplexed when you see human idiosyncrasies interfere with other people's work performance and productivity—as they often will.

SUNNY SHADOWS

Know Thyself means knowing your sunshine. Every human being is endowed with unique talents and gifts, all of which have the potential to make a positive difference in people and/or situations. Used well, your sunshine reflects the special abilities and individual contributions you bring to the team, and often include such gifts as a piercing intellect, creative imagination, harmonizing disposition, or persuasive communication,

Know Thyself also means knowing the point at which your sunshine starts to cast a shadow. The overuse of your sunshine has diminishing returns, often transforming it into an inhibitor of performance. A person with a piercing intellect might spend too much time drilling holes into the thinking of their colleagues, embarrassing or intimidating them in the process. Someone with a creative imagination might spawn too many ideas that are untethered from any remotely practical application. The person with a harmonizing disposition might too quickly subdue the friction that is often needed to shape better ideas or render sounder decisions. A persuasive communicator might hog the limelight or lose sight of when to listen. Notice how all these shadows are outgrowths of the overuse of the sunshine. The journey of self-discovery isn't about identifying your strengths and weaknesses; it's about identifying your strengths and their overuse.

We tend to put leaders on a high pedestal built on inflated expectations. Hardly anyone can live up to such a standard, leaving people who attempt to do so feeling like frauds or failures. As a leader, you'd be much better off embracing all the dimensions of your humanness, including the use, overuse, or misuse of your strengths.

GO DEEPER

Thoroughly examining your life will make you a better and more effective leader. That's why so many leaders are drawn to executive coaching. It's a great way to review and make sense of your reactions and responses to situations and people, so you can make more effective leadership choices in the future. Some leaders go a step further, entering therapy or counseling. Not because they're somehow broken and need to be fixed, but the opposite: because they want to unhook from any anchors they may be dragging from their past so they can act more independently and thoughtfully. My own opinion is that going into therapy is not a sign that you are unwell. It's a sign that you care about your mental wellness. It's about learning to take responsibility for your own life.

You are worth the professional guidance that an executive coach or therapist can provide. If your economic realities prohibit you from hiring a coach or therapist, pick someone with whom you can share the stories that shaped your life. Someone who can gently hold up the mirror when you'd rather avert your eyes. Someone who won't let you get away with hiding from yourself, but also someone who won't let you beat yourself up over past mistakes and regrets. Pick someone who will objectively help you review, make sense of, and integrate the truth of yourself. If you're part of a religious community, perhaps there is a trusted community elder who can guide you. Or maybe you'd be more comfortable visiting counseling.org to evaluate many low-cost and free resources. In the meantime, I'm honored to support your growth and personal exploration as a personal mentor as you read this book.

Deep, guided reflection has two primary benefits. First, you become conscious of the reasons you behave the way you do. You disentangle the influences that your parents had on your thoughts and actions, along with the other influencers who have shaped your beliefs and behaviors along the way. This, in turn, helps you recognize that you aren't as independent as you had supposed, and there may be puppet strings from the past swaying your movement in the world today. Bringing this stuff to consciousness shifts you toward true independence, where your past is no longer controlling your present. When a leadership choice comes your way, instead of reacting out of habituation or history, you respond responsibly based on what the situation warrants, freely, and grounded in your own independent point of view.

The second benefit is that you learn to become an observer of yourself, so that when you're experiencing a frustrating or perplexing situation you can be going through it and processing it at the same time, almost like you're objectively watching it happen to someone else. It's a form of healthy detachment, or disidentifying, so that, again, you can act independently without interference from past imprinting. Developing lasting self-observation skills will have a positive and enduring impact on your overall leadership effectiveness.

INTEGRITY MATTERS

Raise your hand if you don't have any integrity.

I'd be shocked if you actually raised your hand. Not because you'd look silly reading with your arm up in the air, but because pretty much everyone thinks they are a person of integrity. Yet very few people know their own value system. Very few have spent time identifying what they stand for, and what they stand against.

One of the greatest literary works of all time is about a

man traversing a midlife crisis. Written in medieval Italy in the fourteenth century, Dante's Inferno is an epic poem about the effort it takes to close the gap between the person you are and the person you wanted to be. The first canto starts:

Midway upon the journey of our life
I found myself in a darksome wood,
The right road lost, vanished in the maze...

The word "inferno" in Italian means hell. Dante Alighieri, the Florentine genius behind the work, is relating the familiar life experience that many people find themselves contending with eventually. Namely, the hell we fall into when we live inauthentically according to the wants and wishes of others. It's about the consequences of living without a code, unmoored from your own principles. In middle life it is not unusual to find ourselves lost in a dark forest, wondering "How did I get here, and how do I get back to the person I always wanted to become?"

Dante's answer comes down to values. In his view, we get into hell by not having them, and we get to paradise (Dante also wrote Paradiso) by having them, and then living accordingly. The poem, rich with imagery and symbolism, has Dante traveling through the seven gates of hell so that he can get back on a right and truer path. He is aided on the journey by a mentor named Virgil.

One of the most shocking images appears outside the gates of hell, just before Dante and Virgil are set to go inside. They find a group of ghost-like people consigned to marching outside hell's entrance. Dante calls them "shades" because they aren't fully formed people. He also calls them the "uncommitted," explaining that these are the people who never took a stand in life. Their punishment in eternity is to constantly be stung by wasps while endlessly marching behind a banner. And what does it say on the banner? Nothing. Because they stood for nothing in life, they will stand for nothing in eternity. Heaven won't have them, and hell doesn't want them.

It's a powerful metaphor of the fix we get in when we don't embody and uphold a system of values. Avoiding the hell of duplicity, distrust, disloyalty, and all the other interpersonal funk that swirls around people who lack integrity requires having values from which you live and lead.

VALUE VALUES

Integrity is the touchstone of healthy leadership. Developing, nurturing, and guarding your integrity is your first leadership responsibility. Without integrity, your word will mean nothing, and others won't trust you. This is not hyperbole

FIVE FLAGS

Part of what makes taking personal inventory of who you are so critically important is that you can identify what values most drive you and what values you may need to develop to actualize your full leadership potential. Drawing on Dante's symbolism, imagine that you have five flags in front of you. What deeply held value would you put on each flag, and what symbol would you use to convey them? Would you, for example, have a flag dedicated to "family" and draw images to represent your household? Would your flags have words like "honesty," "loyalty," "dependability," or "faith" with related imagery? Being a leader means identifying the flags you're committed to marching behind. This is what it means to lead with integrity. Standing for a set of values keeps you from being one of Dante's ghost-like shades.

and it's a big deal. The trustworthiness of your word means everything when it comes to how willingly people will follow you and how loyal they'll be during hard times. Having integrity means demonstrating a consistency of character and principled living.

Having a bunch of flapping flags and living according to the values they display are two different things. Integrity is a matter of congruency, having a value system and living in accordance with it. If you say you're all about family but you spend all your waking hours at work, you're out of alignment with your family value; you're incongruent. Congruency would mean backing up your value with your actions. I once coached a busy VP who felt guilty about being an absent father. During our coaching conversations, he related how much it meant to him that his own father, despite being a busy business owner, had always made time to attend his JV and high school football games. The VP outwardly claimed that family meant everything to him, yet his own actions only demonstrated neglect. When you are out of alignment with your own value system, your insides will always let you know it. In his case, the VP had a gnawing sense of guilt. He decided to meet with his EVP boss to explain the situation and enlist her support by requesting that he be allowed to leave work a little early two days a week. The EVP, who had children of her own, enthusiastically endorsed the idea. As a result, the VP was able to coach his son's junior football team, put himself back into congruency with his own value system, and stop feeling guilty.

CATALOGUE ADVANTAGES

The conditions you were born into will have a huge impact on the person and leader you will become. It's important to review the story of your formative years and take stock of the ways your upbringing likely impacted how you've developed as a human being. Were you, for example, born into wealth? Did both of your parents go to college? Did your parents stay married and was it a healthy marriage? Was there ample food on the table at every meal? When you got your first job, did you have help getting it? Did you go to public schools or private? Did you go to college? If you did, did your parents pay for it, or did you or they have to take a student loan? Or did you get a scholarship? Academic or athletic? What invisible advantages might you have been born into? Disadvantages? How might lessons from either be put to good use for others?

Privilege is a bit of a charged word these days. Sadly, the word is often wildly twisted and politicized. Some people immediately bristle at the thought that they may have benefitted from invisible life advantages or "tee-ups" that gave them a head start. Some people view privilege as an excuse lazy people use to blame others for their lack of success or to justify their victimhood. Too many people hear the word privilege as an accusation that they didn't work hard, they aren't self-reliant, or that they've been the recipient of gimmies. For them, privilege implies they didn't earn their achievements on their own.

How about we all turn down the temperature on the word? It may help to simply think of privilege as something you have that others could benefit from. That means that privilege isn't just something enjoyed exclusively by rich people or people of one race. I love my friend Gloria Cotton's perspective on this idea. Gloria, whom you will meet in chapter 10, describes herself as pro-inclusionary. She suggests that the lessons some people learn from growing up financially poor can actually be a privilege that people born into wealth rarely receive but could benefit from. People who grow up economically disadvantaged, she explains, are often able to handle significant financial setbacks with less anxiety than wealthier people for whom such setbacks seldom happen. People who grow up with fewer economic means are often versed in how to cutback, be resourceful, delay gratification, and tap into their community as a support vehicle. These valuable life lessons about resourcefulness, resilience, thrift, and endurance often elude wealthier people who rarely, if ever, experience true scarcity. These lessons are the privileges that can come from being poor.

I don't mean to minimize the more traditional connotation of the word privilege. As a white person, I can't recall ever shopping and being followed by security, something that many African Americans experience as a matter of course. I enjoy the privilege of shopping interference-free, largely because of my skin color. I can't allow myself to be blind to that knowledge. Dismissing the experience of others simply because I haven't had their experience is the same as dismissing them. Doing so communicates loudly that they are not important to me or that I think I am more important than them...the very definition of arrogance.

The broader point is that if you aim to be a fair and just leader, you have to have self-awareness, and that awareness can only come from a sober and sometimes painful excavation into your own history.

Thankfully, very few people come from a background where all their achievements were handed to them on a silver platter. By the time you reach your thirties, there's a good chance you have experienced triumph and tragedy, favoritism and bias, decencies and indignities. Most human beings know how intrinsically satisfying it is to achieve something as a result of their own hard work. Most, too, know what it's like to receive a favor that allowed them to bypass the steps that others had to go through to get something. From a leadership standpoint, what matters is that you identify the privileges, advantages, and disadvantages that were part of your own life history and identify ways you can use all of it to serve others.

Dismissing the experience of others simply because I haven't had their experience is the same as dismissing them.

YOU UNITED

I recently watched a YouTube video from 1977 with famed journalist Barbra Walters interviewing country music legend Dolly Parton. It's worth recognizing that Dolly is more than an amazing musician and songwriter who has composed over three thousand songs. She's an outstanding business professional who employs thousands of workers at her Dollywood theme park alone. She is also a philanthropist. In 1995, she launched Dolly Parton's Imagination Library through the Dollywood Foundation. Each month the library donates over 850,000 books to disadvantaged children to promote literacy. So, yes, Dolly is a leader. During the interview, almost insultingly, Walters asks Dolly, "Do you ever feel that you're a joke? That people make fun of you?" Rather than get defensive, Dolly replies, thoughtfully and assuredly, "I am sure of myself as a person. I am sure of my talent...I am secure with myself."

The kind of inner security and confidence that makes Dolly Parton, Dolly Parton, is the same stuff that draws us to her. It's also what results from knowing yourself deeply. To Know Thyself means soberly assessing every aspect of your human nature and coming to terms with who you are. The point isn't to excise the bad parts. There really are no bad parts. Rather, the point is to become a whole, complete, and

Leading since 2000

Kimberlee Curley

VP, Workforce Readiness Consulting Practice Leader, NTT DATA

What's a key leadership lesson that I had to learn the hard way? Authenticity. There was a time in my career when I tried really hard to be like the other leaders around me because they were the ones being rewarded with bigger jobs, promotions, more money. So, I mimicked their swagger and attitude and approach to things. For a while. It was awful—awful for me because acting out of alignment with my values and who I am at my core takes a crazy amount of energy and hurts like hell. It also hurts the very people who have trusted you with leadership. The real truth of that situation is that those people were not great leaders, they were just winning at a game with terrible rules. I pretty quickly decided I didn't want to play that game, and I certainly didn't want to win at it. I've been "me" ever since.

secure person, with a keen understanding of your emotional alchemy. The goal is to be fully comfortable in your own skin. One of the highest compliments that can be said about any human being is "they know who they are." The phrase suggests that you know the core truths about yourself and don't mask them by pretending to be someone other than who you actually are. Self-awareness should ultimately result in authenticity. Others will trust you when the real you is the same as the leader you, regardless of your human imperfections. No one wants to be led by a perfectly fake leader.

THINK NOW/*ACT NOW*

Think Now

What personal achievement are you most proud of? What values or principles helped make the achievement possible?

What is a personal regret you have, or a do-over you'd like? What values or principles did you fail to live?

To what extent have you explored your past? Who are some people, for better and for worse, who impacted who you are today? How might time spent in executive coaching or therapy be useful to you and your leadership?

How would others describe the values you most uphold? What would they say you're "all about"?

What are you "all about"?

What should others know about working with you so that they can be successful?

Act Now

- List your sunshine strengths and the value they bring. Next, list the negative impacts (shadows) that emerge from the overuse of your strengths. Finally, for each sunshine, list the indicators that will help you be aware of when a sunshine might be starting to cast a shadow.
- Do the "Five Flags" activity described earlier. Pinpoint what you stand for and against.
- Drawing on the Five Flags activity, rate each of your values according to how well you live them. Use a 1 to 10 scale with 10 equating with "Perfectly." Identify which values have scores you want to improve and decide on the actions you will take to improve them.
- Think about a leader whom you admire–someone you know or have worked with. Write down what you believe their values to be. Extra credit if you contact them afterwards and ask them what they believe their deepest values to be.

NOTE: Just as a business should take a yearly inventory of its stock, so should you! Consider going on a yearly retreat, even if it's only for a long weekend, to review your Sunshine and Shadows, and take stock of your progression as a leader.

BONUS TIP

All the courageous psychological excavation and reflection involved in knowing thyself should result in gaining clarity about the better person you want to be. In other words, who you are today is the starting point for defining who you want to be tomorrow. Knowing yourself is about taking stock of who you are now. But that knowledge is useful only if it helps you envision—and eventually become—a better, more aware and influential you. This process is like a business taking inventory of its resources and strengths, and then strategically mapping out a future that capitalizes on those strengths while shoring up vulnerabilities. A fancy word businesses sometimes use to describe this envisioning process is futurecasting.

One great way of deciding who you aim to be as a leader, as well as the influence you hope to have on others, is to consider: Who is the leader my team deserves? In other words, start from the needs of those around you, not from what you hope to get out of them. You may find it equally helpful to complete the following statement using a bullet list: The people I am privileged to lead deserve a leader who is...

Your first two-word bonus tip is:

FUTURECAST YOURSELF

CHAPTER 2

MODEL PRINCIPLES

Live the Values You Want Others to Live By

People do as leaders do. Most of the people you lead will mimic your words, behaviors, and attitude. This is not flattery...it's human nature. You do it too. There's a good chance that you now mimic the words and actions of the people who have led you in the past. We learn through mimicry, and we are all mimics of each other. Right this very minute, human beings all over this great big world are mimicking the people who influenced them, while themselves influencing others who will come to mimic them someday. As a leader, you must be conscious of, and intentional with, the power your role modeling has in influencing the behavior of others.

Years ago, I facilitated an offsite meeting with the president of a bank and his senior executive team about whether to modify the bank's dress code. You may find this hard to believe, but there was a time when many professions required employees to dress in their "Sunday best"—suit and tie for men, below-the-knees dresses and pantyhose for women. Then, in the early 1990s, some businesses decided to get a little less stuffy...one day a week. On "Casual Fridays" men could put on their khakis and a polo shirt and ditch their sport coats, and women could wear open-toed shoes and higher-hemmed dresses or pants. Some leaders struggled with the transition, fearing that dressing casually would give the impression the business was lowering its standards.

During the offsite, the president asked, as if he were genuinely interested, to hear the perspectives of his senior executive team. It was quiet at first—as if people didn't feel safe sharing their true perspectives. Finally, someone spoke up, saying, "Shouldn't we dress like our customers? Dressing as we do may be sending the impression that we think we're 'above' them, making them feel like we're looking down at them." The first comment inspired another person to speak up, "I agree, dressing above them is condescending. Plus, many of our customers come during their lunch break from work, and from what I see, many of their businesses are starting to dress more casually. Shouldn't we follow their lead?" Other execs expressed similar thoughts, and as they did, nearly every head in the room was nodding "yes"—except one: the president's.

Before the president weighed in with his opinion, it was clear that his team uniformly supported moving to a Casual Friday dress code. Then, with a small cough of annoyance, the president spoke. "What you all said surprises and disappoints me. Our bank has long prided itself on professionalism, and much of that is projected by what we wear. If there is any business where customers need to feel confident that their investments are being used wisely and maturely, it's ours. We have a fiduciary responsibility to care for people's money! We must project conservatism and intelligence and conformity. Our customers need to know that every one of us will give them the same exact standard of professionalism and that we'll manage their money just as they would. How we dress is the first impression they get of our standards of professionalism."

What happened next taught me the power of leadership role modeling and how easily people will contort their own preferences and opinions to align with a leader—even when they don't truly agree. People started rewinding what they had said before the president spoke. One person said, "Well, when you put it that way, I can see how dressing casually, even one day a week, would send the wrong impression." Another chimed in, "You know, you're right. I hadn't considered that we wouldn't be perceived as good stewards of people's money if our dress suggested that we were 'casual' or 'informal.'" One by one, to a person, everyone backed down and found a way to conform to the leader's opinion. The only person who remained unchanged was the leader himself. It was clear that he wasn't actually interested in hearing people's perspectives, he just wanted to voice his own preferences and make the others yield. It was as comical as it was tragic.

The story of how people get in line with their leader's viewpoint plays out every day throughout the world. Though the situations vary, the overarching theme is the same: groups of individuals come to conform to their leader's preferences. Taking their cues from the leader, some will even adopt the leader's behavioral and communication styles. It's a form of twisted loyalty, mimicry, and sometimes subjugation. Consciously, and more often unconsciously, people will sacrifice their own values and individuality to be clones of the leader. The ease with which people conform to the wants and desires of their leaders, however wanton or craven, has been a potent tool of leadership manipulation throughout the ages.

BE INTENTIONAL

Know Thyself as the title of the first chapter was deliberate. If you are blind to yourself and devoid of self-awareness and self-knowledge, you will also be oblivious to the impact of your values, thoughts, and behaviors on those you are leading. It's a missed opportunity because your leadership

Leading since 2003

Jill Pollack

Chief Story Wrangler, Story Studio Chicago, and Cofounder, Story Mode

Being a leader means making tough choices and trusting your gut. I haven't always done that. Years ago I learned the hard way about waiting too long to fire an employee who had already started to "check out" and I let her behavior affect the other team members. I knew she had to go but kept putting off what I knew would be an awkward and challenging talk. When I finally sat down with her, our conversation moved quickly to how unhappy she had been and what she really wanted to be doing. Even though it was a difficult discussion, I was able to switch from "boss" to "mentor" mode and offer some guidance on building the career she really wanted. I realized that so often, taking someone off the team can be the best thing for everyone involved.

impact becomes random and haphazard. Conversely, when you have thoroughly excavated your personal history and you know who you are, you can be intentional about how you carry and conduct yourself, and therefore about the impact that your role modeling is likely to have on others. Thus, being a good role model follows knowing the stuff inside you worth showcasing.

TAKE CHANCES

Sara Blakely, the founder and CEO of Spanx, an intimate apparel company, views being a role model as a primary leadership responsibility. Sara wrote the foreword to the first edition of my book, *Courage Goes to Work,* and describes how she was taught at a young age the value of taking chances and extending yourself—even to the point of failure. As a child, her dad would ask Sara and her brother the same question on Friday nights at the dinner table: "So, kids, what did you fail at this week?" He'd be disappointed if neither kid could offer a good example. But if they had failed at something, he'd congratulate them by giving them a "high five." Learning to face fear and take risks was reinforced as a life necessity.

Sara has developed a mantra she asks herself when facing a major decision: "Sara, if you weren't afraid, would you do it?" If the answer is "yes," she takes a deep breath and does it. She's conscious of the impact her actions, behaviors, and choices have on those she leads. She explains that when people see her take chances and step up to challenges, they are apt to do so themselves, which provides the engine of innovative behavior that propels successful companies.

She is also intentional about how she responds to mistakes that others make. When people make mistakes by taking risks that move the company forward, she is never disappointed. Instead, as her father did when she was growing up, she gives them a high five!

Sara exemplifies the potency of leader role modeling for advancing an organization's culture and goals. What better way to embody Spanx's mission of "helping women feel great about themselves and their potential" than for the CEO to take chances, step up to challenges, and take occasional failures in stride herself?

MODELING VULNERABILITY

One of the interesting things about leading in general, and role modeling specifically, is that you'll often be in a position of having to role model the behaviors your direct reports aren't yet exhibiting. In other words, leadership often requires that you lead from where people haven't yet arrived. Through your own behavior, you create permission for people to shift theirs, as the following story illustrates.

One of my coaching clients, the head of safety for a construction-related company, wanted to disarm people so that they could have honest conversations about the role of safety in their home and work lives. The company had launched a strategic initiative to rebuild its safety culture after having suffered several jobsite fatalities in the previous five years. The initiative involved everyone in the company attending a series of intensive workshops focused on developing a culture of caring. This represented a substantial shift for the company. Until this initiative was launched, even small mistakes had been met with harsh punishments, which, counterproductively, caused people to hide safety mistakes and near misses. The stiff punishments and the hiding behavior it prompted, ironically, made the construction jobs less safe. The culture of caring that the company was aiming for would involve leaders adopting a less punitive approach when mistakes were made, behaving as teachers and coaches instead of cops and judges. The culture shift would also require changing people's natural impulse to hide mistakes.

An initial goal was to have everyone internalize the responsibility for employing safe practices to ensure that at the end of each job shift everyone returned home in the same shape they had begun the day. Setting a safety culture required having people come to terms with their own relationship to safety, including their personal safety lapses. It's easy for people to point at the company and say, "Things need to be safer!" It's much harder for individuals to ask themselves, "Am I a safe person?" The reality was that a lot of people in the company weren't as safe as they gave themselves credit for being, and part of the aim of the first workshop was to surface that fact. But pointing a finger in people's faces would just inspire resentment and defensiveness. Instead, the safety director kicked off the session by sharing honest stories, most from outside of work, about his own past safety lapses. He also shared something profoundly personal, which you'll learn about shortly, that stemmed from how deeply he internalized it when people were injured on the job. Then he walked to the flipchart where the names of the people who had died over the previous five years were listed. He took time to share personal stories about each person, some of whom had been his friends, while others he had learned about through conversations with their family members.

Throughout the stories, he would get choked up and have to pause to regain his composure. By the end, tears were rolling down his face. Many people in the room, mostly construction workers, were choked up too. It was powerful stuff.

It was also powerful role modeling. After the safety director sat down, people slowly got up and shared their own stories using microphones stationed throughout the large conference room. One person mentioned almost causing an accident because of texting while driving. Another confessed to a habit of guzzling three energy drinks a day to stay awake on the job. Still another related embarrassment at having relapsed with his cigarette habit only three months after suffering a near-fatal heart attack. One person shared that his three-year-old son had climbed a ladder that he had carelessly left up after cleaning his gutters, and the deep shame that had come over him after he had safely carried his son down from the roof. One after another, people shared embarrassing stories about their own safety lapses, many from their personal lives. After getting to this touchtone level of honesty, people were eager to do better. Being a safe company would need to start with being safe people.

It is likely that the safety director was able to inspire such a candid and important conversation because, years earlier, he had been through an important life transformation that had caused him to take stock of his life and reevaluate the impact he wanted to have on others. As he explained during the session, because of his role, whenever injuries at work happened, he would feel it was his fault—as if he had let the company down. The feelings were dramatically worse on the rare occasions when death occurred. All of this, layered on top of already intense work and at-home demands, resulted in his increasingly seeking to ease the pressure with a few stiff drinks at the end of the day. Before long, as he explained, he was abusing alcohol daily, until he hit bottom and his wife filed for divorce. Though he lost his marriage, the divorce was a wake-up call, and he got into Alcoholics Anonymous and started "working the steps." As part of that process, he had worked with a sponsor to take a personal inventory and later make amends to all the people he had harmed through his drinking. He shared the entire emotionally raw story in the conference room that day in hopes that it might be helpful for others to hear. As a result of all the inner work he had done as part of his ongoing recovery, he was perfectly suited to bravely role model the kind of openness and vulnerability that everyone in the conference room would need to exhibit to have the conversations that could transform the culture. His knowing himself allowed for potent and intentional role modeling.

LIVING PRINCIPLES

So much about leadership involves being the best you can be so you can draw out the best in others. Being your best self, as discussed in the previous chapter, requires having a core set of principles that you live by—the stuff that's on your flags, the banners you'll willingly march behind. In the same way that flagbearers whom you admire in your work and life have influenced what's on your flag, others will come to hoist their own flags based on the ones they've seen you fly. Being conscious of the positive impact that you'll have on others by living your principles is important.

In 2018 I coauthored *The Leadership Killer: Reclaiming Humility in an Age of Arrogance* with Captain John "Coach" Havlik, retired Navy SEAL. John and I have been friends since we were teammates on the swimming and diving team at West Virginia University. A few years before writing the book, we had reconnected at an alumni event. When we set out to write our book

I was thrilled because I was sure I'd get some insider knowledge about the global clandestine operations that John had been part of during his thirty years as a SEAL officer. I looked forward to getting the inside scoop about impossible missions where John and the teams he led had, I presumed, snuffed out diabolical dictators bent on world-domination. But every time I pestered John for juicy stories, he'd cut me off at the pass.

In the months John and I worked together on the book, I came to appreciate John's 'core.' He never shared any SEAL secrets because he had sworn an oath not to. But John's core is bigger than oath-taking. It is the inner guidance system that influences how he behaves in the outer world. He displayed his internal value of loyalty outwardly through his abiding commitment to his SEAL teammates and the missions they performed together. If he were to share secrets, it would dishonor them and the work they had done together. In fact, few things angered him as much as former SEALs he called "showboats"—soldiers who would write a book and reveal confidential information, mostly to show how badass they were. John sees this as a breach of everything the SEALs stand for.

A SEAL shouldn't be about himself, John will tell you. He should be about the mission, the team, and quietly doing what's right but hard. SEALs follow a code that has seven statements, reflecting principles that define a standard of conduct. Among them are "Serve with integrity on and off the battlefield," and "take responsibility for your actions and the actions of your teammates." To John, the SEAL Code isn't a bunch of empty platitudes. It informs every aspect of who John is. In all the time we collaborated, I witnessed what it's like to live with a strong inner core. John never told a confidential story. He never once told an off-color joke, and never made a sexist comment. To do those things would do more than dishonor others, they would dishonor him.

When you live by an honorable code, as revealed through your actions and deeds, they'll know they can trust you. Your word will hold real value. People will feel safe because they'll know you won't intentionally harm them, or 'use' them, or treat them unfairly. Equally important is the impact that living your code will have on how others develop and start to live by their own code. Drawing out the best in others starts by reflecting the best of yourself.

GETTING GOOD

Who you are as a leader will greatly impact how people respond to you. This is true whether you are conscious of what you're transmitting or not. As much as people will follow your lead, what they're really following is your character. If you're pensive and anxious, people will be nervous around you. If you are manipulative and shallow, people won't trust you. If you're a cocky showboat, people will talk about your arrogance behind your back. It's behavioral science 101; how you carry yourself will be the stimulus for the response others give. This makes your personhood the single most powerful determinant of how others will respond to your leadership influence. You might as well be intentional about how you carry yourself and the impact you want to have on others. The more you model principles worth upholding, the more you'll be a leader worth following and the more people will follow your lead. Take good care of that inner stuff because it will greatly impact your outer world. Receiving such things as honesty, conscientiousness, fairness, tolerance, maturity, respect, and just plain goodness from others will be much more likely when, through your personhood, you're giving out those things. Being a good leader starts with being a good person, and being a good person inspires goodness in return.

How you carry yourself will be a stimulus of the response you get from others.

THINK NOW/*ACT NOW*

Think Now

If you were to single out a few core virtues that you would most like to guide your life and leadership, what would they be?

How has your own value system been influenced by leaders or influential people you know?

What positive impact do you hope to have on others through your leadership influence? Why is having this impact important to you?

What positive impact do you think your direct reports hope your leadership influence will have on them? Why might having this impact be important to them?

Describe a specific instance where you took deliberate action based on a principle you hold dear.

Describe a specific instance where you failed to uphold a principle you hold dear. What would you do differently if you were to face a similar situation in the future?

Act Now

- Review the Five Flags activity from the last chapter. Refine that answer to draw on what you learned during this chapter.
- Leveraging your work at the end of the previous chapter, create a list of deliberate actions you could take to live your values more visibly.
- Read *Good Comes First: How Today's Leaders Create an Uncompromising Company Culture That Doesn't Suck*, by S. Chris Edmonds and Mark S. Babbitt.

BONUS TIP

Ben Franklin offered this simple suggestion about conscious role modeling in his autobiography. Bookend your day with two powerful questions. At the start of the day ask, "What good shall I do this day?" and at the end of the day reflect on, "What good have I done today?"

Such simple questions, yet so powerful as daily reminders to bring your best to the world. Your two-word bonus has to do with bookending your day by contemplating the good you want your leadership to bring.

Your next two-word bonus tip is:

DELIVER GOODNESS

CHAPTER 3

ASPIRE HIGHER

Continually Lift People, Performance, and Profits

You've got to get better. Everyone does. The torch of self-improvement should burn bright throughout your life. You will never "graduate" as a leader. You will never be granted absolution from the obligation to improve. The people you lead deserve your continuous work on yourself so you can do a better job for them. You're not expected to be perfect, and too much perfectionism will interfere with your leadership (can you say, "micromanager"!), but you are expected to continue refining, shaping, strengthening, developing, advancing, and elevating yourself. You are, and always will be, a work in progress.

EARN IT

Learning to lead and becoming an ever-better leader is hard work. While you might benefit from people's guidance and advice along the way, you're not going to have things handed to you. Even after speaking with leaders you admire, attending online leadership courses, and reading lots of words about two-word leadership concepts, you're still going to get a lot of things wrong along the way. You're still going to have to roll up your sleeves and double down on your commitment to improve as a leader.

People will follow your leadership more willingly when

they know you're busting your hump to do the best job you can. The opposite is also true; when they think you're slow-rolling it, or that things have been handed to you undeservedly, they'll respect you less and question your competency. It's in your best interest to earn your right to lead, every day.

In the last chapter, I told you about my Navy SEAL buddy, retired Captain John "Coach" Havlik, and how he lives by a solid inner core. The last imperative of the SEAL credo he follows captures this idea of reclaiming the right to lead daily: Earn your trident every day.

The trident is the SEAL symbol for their relentless commitment to excellence and is worn on their uniforms over their hearts. It reflects the self-mastery to which SEALs continuously aspire. Unless you're a SEAL, you'll never get to wear a trident over your heart befitting the merits of your noble work. Nonetheless, you've got to honor the privilege you've been given to lead others by continuously working on yourself in a disciplined way.

RESPECT EFFORT

Many of the leaders I work with lead crews on large construction jobs. These are no-nonsense folks leading projects where millions of dollars and lives are at stake. They work on airport runways, interstate highways, bridges and viaducts, water treatment plants, and large commercial buildings, among other things. In the construction world, when someone says they "respect" another person, that respect almost always equates to hard work. Nothing will earn the respect of crew leaders, superintendents, and general foremen as much as a person's work ethic. This is true whether that person works alongside them as a peer, under them as a laborer, or above them as a boss. What matters is whether that person cares enough about the work to show up early and work late when the job requires it?

A lot of leaders start out in positions that are directly related to the most essential work of the organization—typically the work that draws revenue. In construction, for example, a crew leader may start by leading a small crew on a small job, or as a project manager who works closely with the crew leader. Each task performed has a direct impact on productivity and performance. It makes sense that having a strong work ethic would garner people's respect because it makes a tangible impact on the financial health of the organization. As you progress in your leadership career, you'll become increasingly distant from the revenue-generating work and a few steps removed from the people doing it. You'll spend more time in meetings, entertaining clients, developing business, and strategizing about the future. All those things are important, but all those things are practically invisible when compared with the nitty-gritty work that makes money for the organization. To the folks doing the *work* work (versus the *conceptual* work that you'll likely be doing), it'll seem like you're no longer in the trenches with them. When they see you go to a posh location for an offsite business retreat, no matter how hard you are working, they'll question how hard you actually work.

In the construction world, one of the most common complaints I hear from senior leaders is that they miss "the work"—the days when they were (literally) building concrete things. They miss driving down the road with their kids in the backseat and being able to point to a high-rise complex and say with pride, "See that, kids? I helped build that." They miss the work they did before they had to be in meeting after droning meeting reviewing spreadsheets and reports.

You may be years away from this point in your leadership

journey, but it's good to be aware that, eventually, the nature of your work will shift from concrete to conceptual, from tactical to strategic, and from doing to thinking. It's also good to be aware that the most respected senior leaders are the ones who are deliberate about staying connected to the folks doing the "real" work. As the owner of one of the businesses I've worked with said, "We sometimes have round-the-clock work crews who are working in weather conditions that can only be described as brutal. The night that we've got crews working during a blizzard is the night I'm going to show up at the job site trailer with coffee and donuts. I don't care if it's 3:00 a.m. How can I have any respect at all unless I show them the respect that they deserve when they most deserve it?"

You want the people and teams you lead to respect you? The starting place is with your work ethic. It's the most visible way of showing your commitment, and that you don't take your role for granted. Don't slough off!

ADD VALUE

Years ago, I was tasked with typing a client memo for my boss. One of the lines taught me a lot about his mindset, and about leadership in general: We always deliver value far beyond our fees.

I've never forgotten that lesson, and neither should you. The organization you work for, and indirectly the clients you serve, are paying you to deliver value. They want to know that the value they are paying for is worth it. Meaning, they want to know that you are worth the money they are paying you. Your paycheck may seem very removed from the work you're doing, like it magically appears from the organizational apparatus every two weeks, but it reflects what the organization thinks your efforts are worth. You should always aim to be worth more than you're being paid, and you'll accomplish that to the extent you continually increase your skills, knowledge, and influence. At the end of each week, you should slide across the finish line with dirt on your uniform, leaving nothing on the playing field and feeling like you earned every single penny of your paycheck.

One of my clients is a family member in a multi-billion-dollar family-owned business. Some people in that situation skate past the work, comfortably coasting because they know they can get away with it. Others, like my client, take a diametrically opposite approach. They know that others will be scrutinizing them closely to see if they'll take advantage of the privileges their last name might afford. Though my client was already well-established in the company and forty years old, he decided to go back to school and earn his executive MBA. It was quite a commitment, requiring intense study and paper-writing on top of an already huge workload. It meant working on most weekends for over two years and asking his spouse to take on extra parenting duties so he could make everything fit. Why did he do it? Because he felt that the marketplace of the business was changing rapidly, and the added knowledge would help him keep up with those trends, thereby adding more value to his role.

Sometimes adding more value is an outgrowth of proving yourself to yourself. When he completed his E-MBA, with a 4.0 GPA, no less, the exec had a newfound confidence, which he asserted by offering more input in meetings with his colleagues. But, going back to school gave him more than a more confident voice. It helped remove any self-consciousness he secretly harbored about whether or not he had achieved what he had in the company without merit. He had greater clarity about the value he was providing and knew that he could provide this same value to other companies, not just one that bore his last name. He had proven his own worth to himself.

You might be thinking, "Well that's fine and dandy, but the place I work doesn't pay for people to go back to school." That's beside the point. Many leaders go back to school on their own dime. I've known many top-level leaders (including presidents and CEOs) who never went to college but continued to invest in themselves in other ways. I truly hope that your workplace will sponsor your continued education, whether through a formal development program or by subsidizing the costs of going back to school. But what they do has no bearing on your own responsibility to continue to improve. At the very least, initiate conversations with leaders you admire and learn from their stories. Those conversations are a form of investing in your own development. The question you should be asking yourself is, "Am I worth investing in?"

Let me answer the question for you: "Of course you are!" You wouldn't have invested in this book if you didn't think you were, and I wouldn't have written it if I didn't wholeheartedly think so too! Here's something worth knowing: your career, whether you're a leader or not, is your career. When it comes to improving yourself, never use what your organization isn't doing for your development as an excuse to stop improving. Your career will always mean more to you than it does to your organization...or your spouse, or your parents, or anyone else alive. Because it should mean more to you. Why? You already know. Whose career is it again?... that's right: YOURS!

Take charge of your own development. Sure, if you can make a strong plea for your organization to pick up the tab for your development, do so. But you should be prepared to invest in yourself in whatever way you can afford. This is not just hollow author preaching. Two years ago, I flew from my home in Asheville, NC, to Vancouver, British Columbia, to meet with two different leadership experts who are friends of mine. Both have businesses that are a few steps further down the road than mine, and I knew I could learn from them. So, on my own dime, I traveled north to spend a day with each friend, soaking up everything they'd be willing to share with me. Why? So I could add more value to my clients by investing in my own capabilities.

DEVELOP YOURSELF

You matter and so does your ongoing improvement. There are a ton of ways to invest in yourself to add more value to the people and organization you serve and keep earning your right to lead each day. Not everyone has the financial means to put themselves through an expensive leadership program but do what you can. Tap into your local library or watch free YouTube videos or TED Talks. Here are some other development options:

- Take a certificate course or become qualified in a new industry practice.
- Join a professional association to enlarge your network while acquiring additional professional know-how.
- Sign up for a free university course at MOOC.org (MOOCs stands for Massive Open Online Courses).
- Subscribe to a business, industry, or trade-related magazine or podcast (many are free).
- Go on a yearly professional business retreat.
- Get an annual subscription to MasterClass.com and learn from leadership "masters" like Sara Blakely, founder of SPANX; or Anna Wintour, Editor-in-Chief of Vogue Magazine; or Bob Iger, former CEO of Disney.

WORK PRIDE

Early in my career, when I was a new project manager, I was tasked with overseeing the creation of a success-story publication that would detail the value that our clients were receiving for my company's services. At the time, I was working on the largest outsourcing engagement in the history of the world. A Baby-Bell communications company had outsourced their entire IT software function—involving over seven hundred software applications—to the company I worked for. The client was paying my company over $350 million per year as part of a multi-billion-dollar contract. We wanted to make sure the client was clear about the value we were providing, and the success-story project was one way to do this.

As the project lead, I was responsible for leading a small team that would gather success stories from over 250 project managers. Each story had to be catalogued, edited, and verified for accuracy. It would be quite embarrassing to claim any wins that the client could dispute. Thus, everything needed to be irrefutable. The aim was to create an attractively produced, high-quality publication that our own teams could review to become fully educated about our good work across the enterprise, and that we could share with our clients to remind them about the value they were receiving for their large investment.

Before going to press, I wanted to make sure that everything was accurate and clear. So as a final part of the process I had mock versions of the final product created and distributed them to our senior executive team—eight EVP-level people—for review. I also sent a follow-up email giving everyone a two-week deadline.

Two weeks went by. I got nothing.

So I sent a follow-up email reminding everyone of the

importance of the project and letting them know that if I didn't hear from them, I'd be going to press without their input. I gave them a new one-week deadline.

The week went by. Nothing.

Finally, the day before shipping the project off to the printer, one of the senior execs, who had been on vacation during some of the time I had asked for a review, asked to meet with me in a small conference room. Jim was a few years younger than I, but a few rungs higher on the org chart. "Bill," he started, "I was off the last few weeks, but I wanted to give you some input before you ship this off. Turn to page 8…"

Page-by-page, Jim pointed out inaccuracies and flaws. It was striking how many mistakes he had found. When he was done, I said, "Jim, I'm so grateful you took the time to do this. I had sent the project to the senior execs three weeks ago and got no feedback at all." As soon as the words were out of my mouth, he cut me off. "Bill, stop. With a project this consequential, if you aren't getting the attention you need from the higher-ups, it's your fault, not theirs. Do you know how many emails each of us gets a day? This project is important enough that you should have walked into each exec's office and asserted yourself. Look, Bill, this is your project. People associate it with you. Though there is no name on the front of this publication, it might as well have your signature on it. You need to approach it like it does. The quality and accuracy of this reflects on you."

Jim Bailey, who is now the CEO of the Americas Strategic Business Unit of Capgemini, a digital transformation and technology consulting firm, wasn't being a jerk. That wasn't his style or his motive. He was taking the time to teach me about pride of authorship. I've never forgotten that conversation or the lesson I drew from it.

As you become more seasoned, you'll start to evaluate the

people who work under your direction by asking "Do they give a rip?" The criterion of give-a-rippedness separates people who hold themselves accountable, are quality-minded, and have a strong work ethic from those who don't. There's a good chance giving a rip was one of the criteria your bosses used to gauge your deservedness before they moved you into your first leadership role.

As a new leader, especially, you must care deeply about the quality of your work and your growing reputation. That caring will show up in your work ethic, and it will ultimately determine the degree of success you achieve. When you care about the work you do, and the people you impact through your work, you'll never stop wanting to improve. That's called drive. And that's what it means to Aspire Higher.

THINK NOW/*ACT NOW*

Think Now

Who is someone you consider to have a great work ethic? Is your general opinion about this person positive or negative?

What is the last investment you made to develop yourself? What is the next investment you're willing to commit to so you can become even more effective as a leader?

When was the last time you were genuinely proud of the work you did because of the quality of your craftsmanship? What is the next task or project where having pride in workmanship will be important?

Act Now

- Read this blog post by my friend retired Navy SEAL officer Mark Divine, founder of SEALFIT: sealfit.com/the-mark-divine-blog-earn-your-trident-every-day/.
- Assuming that "10" is "Outstanding," how do you rate your current work ethic on a scale of 1 to 10?

- How would the people you lead rate your current work ethic?
- List all the ways you are adding value to the organization you serve. Then create a new list and identify ways to add even more value.
- Act on the investment you committed to in the Think Now section above.

BONUS TIP

Early in my career, I sat down with a leader in the company where I worked and asked what she felt was the key to career success. Her answer surprised me.

Twenty years later, I was sitting in the office of a billionaire owner of a successful business and I asked him the same question. He gave me the same surprising two-word answer: Take notes!

When you're meeting with people, take copious notes about the interesting things you learn, the commitments that you and others make, and whatever else you hear worth documenting. Not only will you have an accurate and up-to-date track record worth referencing, but you'll also be showing people—in a visible and tangible way—that what they say, and the work you're all doing together, matters. Taking notes is a sign of respect for both yourself and others.

Your next two-word bonus tip is:

TAKE NOTES

CHAPTER 4

GAIN CONTROL

Be Better for Everyone Through Self-Mastery

Soon after moving into a leadership role, you discover that what you thought a leader's job would be and what it is are two different things. Before becoming one yourself, you might have envied those in leadership roles. After all, instead of working out of a cubicle, they had roomy offices. Instead of working alone on a spreadsheet, they were gathered in the conference room making heady decisions while an underling took notes. Instead of passively sitting in the audience during the town hall, they got to present a compelling future to everyone. The work you watched them doing seemed more varied, impactful, and important. You envied their bigger titles, offices, and salaries!

While you may enjoy a honeymoon period where your new leadership role is enjoyable, you'll quickly discover that it comes with pressures from all sides. There will be leaders above you impatiently pressuring you to get more and more results while giving you fewer and fewer resources. There will be people reporting to you who pressure you for more attention, compensation, and time off. There will be peers competing against you for a bigger portion of limited supplies or that next promotion. You'll have loved ones at home wondering if you'll ever again be the easygoing person you used to be, while yearning for your full presence. You'll pressure yourself to live up to everyone else's expectations to relieve the pressure. It's a fool's errand.

Leadership is hard. Period. Full stop.

Yes, as a leader you'll have more freedom in how you use your time, more interesting challenges to work on, more influence over the direction of people's careers, and more involvement in the big decisions that will impact the organization. All those enjoyable things won't add up to more enjoyment. They mostly add up to more stress.

The entire first section of the book has been devoted to Leading Yourself. This chapter is about managing yourself by gaining control of your stress, time, and attitude.

WHAT MAKES LEADERSHIP SO HARD?

When you move into a leadership role for the first time, you quickly discover that the job isn't all sunshine and rainbows. Leadership is dang hard! Here's why:

Unpredictable People. You lead people, and people are fickle, quirky, and often petty. On occasion, even experienced employees will act childish, like grown-up toddlers wearing bigger clothes and sporting larger and more fragile egos. Sure, they can be smart, passionate, and upstanding, too. The problem is unpredictability. On any given day, in any given work situation, it is hard to predict which people are going to act like adults and which are going to act like whiny, sniveling, irritable babies. Some people will respond to your feedback receptively; others will get defensive or stew with resentment. And some days you'll be the biggest baby in the room—usually when you think everyone around you is acting infantile.

Relentless Demands. You're only deemed successful as a leader if you get results. The drive to produce results is incessant. No matter how well you do this quarter, or with this project, or with this customer, you'll be expected to do more and better next time. Your reputation is always on the line. The pressure is multiplied by the fact that people are counting on you to not let them down. Your organization holds you to the same expectation. And when the needs of your direct reports conflict with the needs of the company, you'll be caught in the vise of competing demands.

Uncomfortable Change. Leadership has everything to do with creating, managing, and effecting change, which, by definition, is uncomfortable. People are comfort-preferring creatures. That said, human beings (and organizations) don't grow in a zone of comfort. We grow, progress, and evolve in a zone of discomfort. The harsh reality is that your job as a leader is to nudge people into doing things outside of their comfort zones—and into their discomfort zones. That means your job is to sometimes make people uncomfortable. That discomfort, though, must be absorbable. Toxic levels of discomfort provoke fear and paralysis. But not enough discomfort breeds complacency. The goal is to help people stretch toward higher goals and standards without overwhelming them.

No Cavalry. Self-reliance is a hallmark of strong leadership. You'll sometimes feel under siege from the volume and intensity of the challenges you're facing. Regardless, you'll be expected to bring them to resolution—without the aid of a handbook. Leadership can be a lonely endeavor. The cavalry isn't coming to save you, and you'll often be forced to grope your way through, often making things up as you go along. You'll often feel like a fake on the inside while straining to portray confidence on the outside.

You're "It." Leaders are not like everybody else. The reason that people don't put in the same obnoxious hours you do, don't view all tasks as urgent, don't snap to attention when tasked with a directive, and don't deliver twenty-four-carat quality is that they shouldn't. Neither should you. But often you do, mostly to the detriment of their results and your health. Leaders often get in their own way by being overly judgmental, holding people to unrealistic standards, and caring more for results than for people. You'll be blind to all of this, of course. Most direct reports won't have the courage to tell you about your contribution to the insanity.

MAXIMUM OVERDRIVE

My company was once hired to develop a leadership program for a fast-growing communications company headquartered in the Southwest. The program consisted of leadership "summits" where we spent a day every other month focused on

Leading since 2013

Katherine Fishstein

National Accounts Department Manager, IES Communications

One lesson I've learned the hard way is that I cannot do it all alone. Working harder does not necessarily mean greater success. Stepping back, delegating, developing, and supporting those on my team instead of trying to carry it all myself is definitely more likely to result in greater growth and success as a team.

an important aspect of leadership. One of the workshops focused on Leading Culture, which was devoted to helping the emerging leaders identify the company's own unique culture, and to having them consider what aspects of the culture no longer serve the company well and might need to shift. Interesting discussions ensued, and one word started surfacing again and again: redlining.

To a person, everyone enjoyed being part of a fast-growing company. They loved winning work back from bigger and more established competitors and working with marquee clients. They felt loyal to the company leaders and appreciated their openness to forward-moving ideas. They liked being part of a company where you could receive more responsibility and more opportunities to make more money, rather than at some of their competitors where younger people had to "wait their turn." There was an entrepreneurial energy that felt electric, like everyone was on a winning team. All of that was uber-energizing. But...

Everyone also felt like they were maxed out. The fury of incoming orders and the ridiculous workload each order created felt all-consuming. It felt like all the success the company was enjoying was untenable. More than one person used the word "redlining" to describe the experience—as if each leader had the throttle all the way open and every day the company's RPMs were deeper into the red zone and the engine was about to blow. People were at once energized, exhausted, and...terrified. They were indeed experiencing redlining!

Redlining: An unsafe, unhealthy, unsustainable condition whereby a leader and/or their team are over-worked and under-resourced for unreasonable amounts of time.

TERMINAL REDLINING

Redlining feels fun. Until it doesn't. Stress must be managed. By you. If you don't manage it, you'll do damage to your leadership impact and your own health. Some years ago, I was coaching the president of an Atlanta-based digital customer experience company. I liked Kevin, the president, a lot. He was just a really good guy: a leader, a family man, and someone trying to bring some good into the world. In addition to being a devoted husband and father of three young girls, he and his wife had made several mission trips to Solai, Kenya, where they served orphan children and helped establish a water utility so the village could have clean water. I mean, really good guy, right?

Whenever Kevin and I met, he would talk about his personal and professional lives with equal passion. He knew, though, that he was out of balance in favor of work and that the imbalance was taking a toll on his well-being. We touched on the topic during each coaching session, and most sessions would end with his identifying actions that he planned to put in place to take better care of himself and spend more time with his family. Frequently, though, when we'd meet again and check in on the promises he had made to himself, he hadn't kept them.

I've worked with a lot of leaders like Kevin over the years, wonderful human beings who suffer from self-neglect, always putting others before themselves. They are deeply dedicated to the people they serve and the responsibilities entailed in serving them. It's as if they work according to a long mental list of all the people and responsibilities they are dedicated and obligated to but their own names are nowhere to be found on the list. Like so many other leaders, Kevin struggled with how to make himself a priority.

As a reminder to shift more of his attention to his family, whom he adored, he kept a picture in his office that one of his daughters had drawn for him when she was young. It was an image of Kevin's wife and the three girls standing outside smiling in the sunshine with their dog. But I noticed that something important was missing. When I asked Kevin why he wasn't standing with the stick-figure family, he said, "That's why I love the image and why it reminds me to make more time for my family. Look up in the sky. See that airplane flying toward the sun? Now see that itty bitty hand waving from the plane? My daughter said that's me...because I'm always leaving on business trips." Ouch.

I wish Kevin's story had ended differently. I wish he had achieved the work/life balance he yearned for. If nothing else, let Kevin's story be a warning to you that redlining can turn into flatlining. While entertaining clients at a golf outing at the famed East Lake Golf Club in Atlanta, Kevin had a massive heart attack and died. He was 47 years old.

PERSONAL FIDELITY

As you progress in your leadership career, it will be increasingly important to make yourself a priority. This doesn't have to come at the expense of all the people, responsibilities, and goals to which you are obligated. You can faithfully serve all those things while also making yourself a priority. The term I use with leaders I coach is Personal Fidelity. The word fidelity has to do with deep devotion, loyalty, and trust. The word is most often used to reflect our dedication to others, such as our fidelity to our spouse and loved ones. The English translation of the Latin phrase Semper Fidelis means "always faithful" and Semper Fi, of course, is the motto of the U.S. Marine Corps, reflecting their abiding loyalty and commitment to their brothers- and sisters-in-arms. The word fidelity, though, isn't confined to faithfulness to others. You'll be an even more effective leader if you also give it to yourself.

Leaders like Kevin are uncomfortable making themselves a priority. To them, focusing on themselves seems self-centered, which, philosophically, goes against the first law of leadership: It's not about you, it's about the people you're leading. But Personal Fidelity isn't about selfishness or conceit. It is simply a recognition of the importance of self-respect and that you'll take better care of others when you first take better care of yourself.

SELF-CARE

Self-care doesn't require selfishness; it requires a starting point. One manager I know took it upon herself to lead an 8:00 AM yoga class three mornings a week. She knew she wanted to take better care of herself and thought that other people in the company felt the same way. She also figured that it would be easier to hold herself accountable to working out if she were joined by a support network of others. At first only a handful of other women showed up. Slowly, drawn in by the sound of laughter coming from the training room, other women joined. Before long, several men started showing up, a few of whom took extra ribbing for their lack of stretching prowess.

Self-care also requires the personal discipline to prioritize yourself. The president of one company I work with ducks out to take a 90-minute lunch a few days a week so that he can take a cycling "spin" class. He notes how the intensity helps him release stress and makes him better able to handle the stressors that the second half of the workday inevitably bring. At first, he was self-conscious, worried that people would know that he was taking a longer lunch. What helped him get over that was the fact that his job often required him to work past dinner and on occasional weekend days. He knew the various ways he added value to the organization, and how taking care of himself would just add to that value by making him less stressed out in the afternoons.

DETONATION DEFUSED

In addition to the negative health impacts of unmanaged stress is the contorting effect it has on your otherwise professional behavior, causing you to be irritable, quick-triggered, or downright nasty. I once worked with a project manager named Duane who had gotten scathing feedback on a 360-degree feedback survey. Such surveys involve being evaluated by your boss, peers, and direct reports, and include objective data (such as continuum averages), as well as qualitative responses to insightful questions. The survey was administered while Duane was shouldering the largest project he had ever led...and it wasn't going well. He was under tremendous stress, which he was externalizing to everyone around him in the form of abrasive behavior. On the survey, people collectively rated his leadership style a two out of five, with five equating to "outstanding." Worse were the words that people used to describe Duane's leadership, which included "hot-tempered," "edgy," "unapproachable," and "explosive."

One comment really stung. "He has to remember that he works for people, and people have feelings. They have to know that he trusts them to make decisions and that he'll cover their backs if something goes wrong. People need to know that he won't publicly take their heads off when they bring up sensitive topics in meetings and that he'll discuss them privately. He's actually a winner, and people will always want to work for a winner as long as they're treated fairly."

During our work together, Duane noted how he used to be a competitive athlete but his work demands caused him to get out of shape. He hadn't worked out in two years, and at lunch, he was prone to scarfing down a juicy mega-burger so he could quickly get back to work. We talked about what self-care would look like for him, and the benefits it would have on his leadership impact and well-being. We talked about the idea of Personal Fidelity and how upholding it is a sign of self-respect. He committed himself to choose a salad three days a week, and to taking a morning run at the job site where he could shower afterwards. He made other commitments too, mostly focused on subduing his quick temper. Unlike the prior story about Kevin, this one has a happier ending. At a pivotal point in his life, and still early in his leadership journey, Duane made real and enduring changes related to self-care. He got in shape, fell in love, got married, had children, and his career progressed. The "explosive" project manager is now a business group leader who leads an entire program (comprising many teams) and oversees a book of business worth close to a billion dollars.

SELF-CARE OPTIONS

What about you? What would self-care look like and what positive impact would it have on your leadership? Here are three low-investment, high-return ways of practicing self-care, reducing stress, and demonstrating Personal Fidelity:

Get Outdoors: There are over 6600 state parks in the United States, and some 423 national parks. The beauty of getting outdoors is, well, the beauty. And the fresh air. Nature has a calming effect on our senses, helping us put things in perspective. Nature, like life itself, follows rhythms and patterns; things are in a constant state of being born, growing, weathering storms, suffering calamities, and sprouting again. When you step into nature you step into an ancient and ongoing universal story—of birth, growth, virility and fertility, vibrancy, equilibrium, decline and decay, death, and perpetual rebirth. Take solace in knowing that your life is a finite chapter in a larger timeless narrative. Reconnecting with nature affirms that, no matter how heavy the weather, hope and life spring eternal.

Go Walking: Could any physical activity be easier? All you've got to do is put one step in front of the other! Check out AmericaWalks.org if you need convincing of the benefits. My advice would be to ditch listening to podcasts or music on your walk, and don't "work" on yourself. Just let your thoughts wander and take notice of the creative inspirations that start to surface. The point is to let your stress dissipate. Leadership coach and philanthropist Jacquelin Schiff says, "The best remedy for a short fuse is a long walk."

Eat Healthily: Even fast-food places have healthy options these days. Instead of fatty fare, why not choose egg whites, grilled chicken, a wrap sandwich, or salad? Heck, even not choosing the Godzilla-sized Euphoria Meal would be a healthier choice, right? For extra credit, try snacking on healthy stuff you truly enjoy throughout the day, be it carrots, peanuts, celery, or an occasional stick of beef jerky!

CATCH EDDIES

Today's furious business environment, and the pressures it comes with, has accurately been described as permanent whitewater; tumultuous rapids with water crashing over big boulders. Whitewater rafters and kayakers rate the difficulty of rivers according to classes, with Class I being tame and Class VI being treacherous and nearly impossible to navigate. As a leader, you'll often feel like a rafting guide, leading your team through whatever class of problem the day's work conditions throw at you. Some days will be tame, other days will feel uncontrollable like you're paddling down a Class V river at flood stage.

What all seasoned raft guides and whitewater kayakers know is that along the river's edge, and outside of the swift-moving current, there are calm spots where the swiftness of the downstream current creates a gently moving upstream alcove called an eddy. You'll often hear rafters and kayakers yell, "Catch that eddy!"—which means "Grab that safe spot!" Eddies are where you catch your breath, get rehydrated, and patch your bones before moving back into the swift-running current. Each eddy is unique. Some are small and barely big enough for one kayak—called micro-eddies. Others are hidden behind giant boulders smack dab in the middle of the river, where the water crashes around both sides of the rock, forming a sort of V where the eddy is the space in between the two wakes created by the waterlines that shoot around each side of the rock. The more difficult the class of river, the more critical it is to scout for the eddies you can catch as you cascade down the river.

Using whitewater as a metaphor, it's essential that you learn to catch eddies whenever and wherever you can. Were you to spend your entire day paddling down fast whitewater, you'd burn out quickly, becoming a danger to yourself and everyone around you. Yet a lot of leaders do just that, equating productivity with time spent at work, staying on the river, day in, day out, regardless of how high and fast and dangerous the river is. Don't do that. Don't book back-to-back Zoom meetings without scheduling breaktime (a form of eddy) in between. Don't hold off on eating lunch until it's 2:30 PM and then scarf it down in 15 minutes while working at your desk, using "I'm just too busy" as your excuse. Grab some sanity whenever you can, especially when your workflow is moving rapidly. As a matter of self-respect and self-care, schedule "me" time, even if it's only for twenty minutes between meetings.

A final word on eddies. One of the most dangerous and destabilizing places to be on the river is in the eddy line. That's where the fast-moving downstream whitewater runs against the slow-moving upstream eddy and its flatwater alcove. The eddy line undulates fiercely, resembling boiling water. To get safely into the eddy alcove, rafters and kayakers must paddle aggressively all the way into the safe harbor, lest the eddy line grabs them by its rip current and flip them upside down. There's a metaphor worth considering here too. Don't be half-assed in your efforts to grab some work/life balance. When you are, both of your worlds get a little topsy-turvy. When you're at work, paddle hard. When you've blocked out some protected eddy time, paddle all the way into the tranquil harbor and let work go fully. No checking your emails. No text messages. No phone calls on your front porch out of earshot of your waiting family. Get out of the eddy line! But for the good of your own sanity, do catch eddies!

MASTER TIME

If there's one thing that senior leaders have in common, it's mastery over how they use their time. It's hard to progress into an executive-level position without being time-efficient, which requires having a high degree of time consciousness. Meaning, you must have a carefully honed internal sense of how much time you've used, how much time you're currently using, and how much you're going to need to use as you progress through each of the day's meetings, interactions, and obligations. You should be able to intuitively sense this without having to look at your watch.

Mediocre leaders are time-oblivious, as if their mental time sensors have been lobotomized. They are constantly running late, creating a runway of lateness behind them as everyone becomes stuck waiting for their direction. The cost of their unprofessionalism rarely occurs to them. Nor are they aware of how easily the cost could be mitigated if they simply used their time more wisely. Time obliviousness is not only unprofessional and costly it's also just plain disrespectful. It suggests that, down deep, they think they're too important to be hemmed in by time constraints, and that others will just have to wait.

While disrespectful, time mismanagement is quite common during the early parts of one's leadership career. Often, it's connected to not yet having learned how to delegate, or not being comfortable doing so. You may have gotten promoted into your leadership role because you were a highly productive and reliable self-performer. Now you're leading a team of people, and, early on, you still equate success with personal output. So you try to know everyone's job more than they do, sometimes even taking on tasks they are responsible for. What often ends up happening is that you get so overwhelmed that you are forced to learn how to delegate out of sheer desperation—you capitulate, surrendering to the fact that you can't do it all yourself and the knowledge that you're robbing your direct reports of the chance to be capable, responsible, and self-reliant. Until you get to this point, your leadership career will be stunted. You won't be able to progress until you learn how to delegate, a topic we'll address in more depth in chapter 9, Nurture Talent.

I once coached a division manager named Frank who was running himself ragged trying to do too many things on his own. Through our work together, we developed a tool that I've since used with many other leaders who wanted to get a better handle on how they use their time. Frank and I call it Time Gapping. First Frank guesstimated how much of his time was spent being productive (stuff that impacts revenue), and how much was nonproductive (administrivia). He started by estimating that he was 75 percent productive and 25 percent nonproductive. Next, he listed all his major obligations on the left side of a piece of paper, being careful not to get too granular. Major obligations were assumed to cover a lot of tiny tasks underneath them. The items he listed included:

Division Manager Obligations
Reviewing estimates/proposals
Writing/sending change orders
Personal development
Working with field personnel
People development
Client relationships
Corporate responsibilities

Next to each item, he estimated the amount of time he currently allocated to the respective obligation, factoring in that all items need to add to 100%.

Division Manager Obligations	**Current Allocations**
Reviewing estimates/proposals	23%
Writing/sending change orders	35%
Personal development	6%
Working with field personnel	9%
People development	10%
Client relationships	9%
Corporate responsibilities	8%
Total	100%

BONUS TIP

Remember, what's going on inside of you usually gets transmitted out. If your brain is cluttered with piles of information that you're trying to keep track of, and, if you sometimes feel like a complete mess on the inside, guess where it will show up? On your desk! The less internally organized you are, the more likely your desk looks like a complete disaster. And why would anyone want to be led by someone who can't even keep their own desk straight? Why would anyone want to be led by, or have confidence in, someone who is outwardly proving that they are a complete scattered mess?

Just as your insides affect your outsides, it works the other way around too. One of the quickest ways to regain a sense of order and control is to clean up your workspace. Do it. Get organized and clean up your act.

Your two-word bonus tip is:

TIDY UP

CHAPTER 5

PRACTICE HUMILITY

Prevent Hubris by Keeping Your Ego in Check

As long as there have been leaders there have been people kissing their rear-ends. The manipulative art of brown-nosing has won the favor of rulers and despots, generals and chiefs, high-priests, and priestesses throughout the ages.

It feels good when the people you're leading fawningly agree with your decisions, affirm and parrot your opinions, and enthusiastically carry out your directives. Some leaders start to surround themselves with yes-people, misjudging sycophantic fealty with genuine loyalty. While it feels nice when your direct reports massage your ego by telling you how smart you are, don't get sucked into being sucked up to. You don't want to be manipulated by lickspittles who win your favor through false flattery. You don't want direct reports who ingratiate themselves by kissing your backside but don't actually have your back. You'll be far better off surrounding yourself with confident people whose strengths offset your deficiencies, and who are loyal enough and courageous enough to let you know when you're about to make a boneheaded decision.

All this applies to how you interact with your boss, too. Few things are as noticeable and flagrantly embarrassing as watching someone currying the boss's favor through groveling. Treating your boss respectfully should never come at the expense of your own self-respect. Don't demean yourself. Don't brown-nose. Keep your nose clean.

LEADERSHIP EXPLOITATION

The power and privilege that accompanies the role of a leader can be massively seductive. There is a tendency for rank-and-file employees to put leaders on a pedestal, treating them as special. Leaders are afforded much more behavioral latitude than everyone else. This latitude grows as the leader advances. It starts out small, such as letting the leader sit at the head of the table or presuming that the leader will kick off the meeting. Over time, the behavioral latitude can result in a greater imbalance between the leader ("superior") and those being led ("subordinate"). Seasoned leaders, for example, can walk into a meeting late without having to offer a good excuse. Likewise, they can interrupt people without their rudeness being challenged, skirt around rules, or exempt themselves from processes to which others are bound. The specialness with which leaders are treated isn't hard to witness. When you moved into your first leadership role, for example, you may have noticed being treated differently than before you were designated a leader. Everything about you was the same...except the perceived importance of your role. The danger sets in when you start to believe that you are more important.

When people at lower levels treat you as special, you may start to exploit the invisible privileges that join that specialness. You may start to treat direct reports more impatiently, dismissively, abruptly, or obnoxiously. Have you ever had a direct report come to your office space with a request while you keep on typing at your computer? Would you do the same thing if the person walking into your space was your boss? Heck no...your boss is too special to be treated that way!

You see what I'm getting at?

By this stage in your career, you've likely had a boss who exploited the privileges that come with being in a leadership role by mistreating you and others, mostly through intimidation. At first blush, you might think that no leader in their right mind would use intimidation to impel people to get work done. It seems like the surest way to lose the confidence of those being led. The sadder truth is that leaders use intimidating behavior to exploit their role because it works. Let me say that again: intimidation works. How so? It creates the illusion of a friction-free environment. When people are afraid of a leader, they won't question or challenge them. Instead, they'll shut their mouths, put their heads down, tether themselves to their keyboards, and get work done without outward complaint. In other words, intimidation is efficient. It requires no intelligence, skill, or finesse. All it takes is being a blunt force object.

While rudeness and intimidation have efficiency payoffs, those payoffs are short-lived and diminishing. Exploitative leadership has a shelf life. Just because intimidating behavior successfully shuts direct reports down doesn't mean they aren't stewing with resentment. That resentment will be like hot embers burning away whatever genuine loyalty the obnoxious leader once had. And without loyalty, a leader's failure is inevitable.

DANGEROUS OVERCONFIDENCE

What we're talking about here, of course, is ego. More specifically, we're talking about the dangers of an inflated ego and how the natural spoils that come with the job of a leader, potentially, can act as a sort of atmospheric helium, swelling the leader's ego and sense of specialness. Subtle at first, ego inflation eventually oversaturates healthy confidence until it becomes poisonous arrogance, and hubris starts to rule. Instead of applying their unique talents toward the pursuit of opportunities that benefit the people they're serving, their concern shifts to how they can use their position to benefit themselves. The entire point of leadership, to leave people and the organization better off than the leader found it, becomes inverted. Now it's all about the leader.

In *The Leadership Killer* written with my coauthor John "Coach" Havlik, the Navy SEAL officer, we detailed hubris as the single deadliest leadership contaminant, and the source of nearly every despicable act done by egomaniacal leaders throughout the ages. "Hubris" is an ancient Greek word that encompasses dangerous overconfidence, abuse of power, and taking pleasure out of humiliating others.

WHAT HUBRIS KILLS

MISSION: Leaders and followers are goal-focused creatures. Having a clear and compelling mission has a unifying effect, lifting people above petty self-interests. Hubris does the opposite. It convinces leaders that their wants and desires stand supreme. Satisfying the leader's own interests IS the mission when hubris is winning. The actual mission gets subverted and becomes a distant priority.

MORALE: It is a leader's job to foster healthy working relationships between teammates. The leader needs to build spiritedness among the team (esprit de corps). When followers come to believe that they are just the machine parts a leader is using to build a monument to him- or herself, morale plummets.

PERFORMANCE: People work well and hard for a leader they admire. The reverse is also true. Performance suffers when followers believe the leader is more hell-bent on getting results or gratifying their own ego than bettering peoples' lives.

LOYALTY: Ask yourself, who would you be more likely to give your loyalty to: a leader who inspired you with courage, sought and valued your ideas, created opportunities for you to grow, and was there when you needed them, or someone who didn't? Followers are loyal to leaders who are loyal to them. A hubristic leader is only loyal to themselves.

ETHICS: A leader is supposed to uphold and embody high ideals and worthy values. The most venerated leaders are people of good character, whose influence grows to the extent that they enrich the lives of others, elevating them to higher personal and professional standards. Hubris, conversely, seeks to magnify and accelerate the leader's moral decay so that, through the power of role modeling, others begin to compromise their own ethics, too.

REPUTATION: As a leader, your reputation will be built on the results you get and the people whose lives you impact during the time they're getting results on your behalf. Leadership is always about producing benefits for, and satisfying the needs of, those being led. But hubris redirects your attention away from others and on to the satisfaction of your own needs and wants. You won't go very far if the only one who thinks highly of you is you.

LEGACY: The costliest impact of hubris is the sheer loss of potential for all the good that could have been done—and all the lives the leader could have positively impacted—had the leader not become drunk with power...The potential to inspire new generations of leaders is snuffed out.

RIGHTSIZED CONFIDENCE

Don't worry, I know you're a good person. I wrote the book just for you, right? All I'm saying is you have to be on guard against the natural seductions that come with being in a leadership role. The spoils of leadership can spoil you. I've seen good and decent people dismantle their entire ethical scaffolding, imploding their careers and personal life in the process. One leader I know was progressing quickly in the company he worked for, to the pleasure of his bosses. He was admired as a go-getter, someone who could be counted on to deliver substantial results, and a faithful churchgoer, presumed to be of unquestioned integrity. But with each promotion his ego swelled. Before long, he moved into the top spot of the regional office, which became a sort of kingdom where he was the ruler. Hubris had hijacked his leadership... and ethics. Unbeknownst to others in the office, he started having an affair with a young new hire. Then, also on the sly, he incorporated his own business and started bidding on work...against the company he worked for. The ego has a way of creating a false sense of invincibility, and the leader figured he'd be able to cloak the identity of the newly incorporated business and his association with it. But he was wrong. He was fired the day his duplicity was discovered. His wife fired him soon after.

My aim in telling you all this is to protect you from yourself. Not because I doubt that you're a good person but because I've seen good people move into leadership roles and then become twisted into thinking they were extra-special because they were treated as such. Confidence is absolutely essential to good leadership; overconfidence is absolutely dangerous to it.

I don't just want you to become a good leader. I want you to stay a good leader. A host of factors impact the longevity and success of an enduring leadership career, including having foresight about the future and a vision to carry it out, being able to enlist others and inspire them to do great work, developing a track record of decisiveness and taking calculated risks, and developing a strong professional network that enables you to create new opportunities. All of these will quickly become insignificant if your ego balloons with hot air. Humility is an overlooked but oh-so-essential leadership characteristic. Gaining humility requires staying vigilant to the early warning signs that your ego is becoming overinflated. Below are ten early warning signs that your ego may be on the verge of corrupting your integrity:

EGO INFLATION *(10 EARLY WARNING SIGNS)*

1. You've got a short fuse when you don't get your way or when others make mistakes.
2. You feel envious when others are recognized for their contributions.
3. You are too easily offended, especially when you perceive that others are disrespecting your authority.
4. You often feel slighted or that you're not getting your fair share. You're in a perpetual state of grievance.
5. You visit your favorite social media sites a lot, not to see what's going on with others, but to check on the status of your posts and how many "likes" and positive reactions they've gotten.
6. You rarely, if ever, ask for feedback about your leadership and how it could be improved.
7. You love winning, even in inconsequential competitions such as games with your children.
8. You spend more time with the bosses and higher-ups than you do with your direct reports.
9. You fixate on your compensation and on getting more.
10. You use "I" more than "we" in meetings and team conversations.

When it comes to the importance of keeping your ego in check, and the dangers that emerge when you don't, consider the warning of author Anne Lamott in her excellent book on creativity, *Bird By Bird*, "Whenever the world throws rose petals at you, which thrill and seduce the ego, beware. The cosmic banana peel is suddenly going to appear underfoot to make sure you don't take it all too seriously, that you don't fill up on junk food."

PURPOSEFUL HUMILITY

Humility can be a hard thing to assess. If you ask someone to rate themselves on humility, and they choose "very humble," it seems contradictory, right? Plus, your ego will never be permanently subdued, no matter how modest, humble, and gracious you are as a human being. Ego, which in both Latin and Greek means "I," will always be vehemently and venomously quick to defend you, compete for you, protect you, and love you. That's the ego's job. It's like a private bodyguard made of your own DNA, a twin absorbed solely by self-interest. To some extent, it's good to have such a blindly loyal defender in your corner but it needs to be under your direction...not the other way around. How? By remaining vigilant to the signs of ego-swelling listed above, and by adhering to a disciplined practice of ongoing ego management and humility maintenance. Below are eight ways to do that.

EIGHT WAYS TO PRACTICE HUMILITY

1. Reflection Check: Each morning you need to be able to look at your own eyes in the mirror without embarrassment, shame, or self-consciousness. Your eyes are the day's first clue as to whether yesterday left some ego messes, often in the form of damaged relationships, that need cleaning up. If you find yourself averting your eyes, you probably left a sizable mess.

2. Deputize Truth Tellers: Given the ego's propensity to see itself as blameless, it's not enough to check yourself. Instead, deputize others by giving them permission to question you when your actions seem out of step with your values. Pick people who have a history of giving it to you straight, out of advocacy, not malice. These people may be family members, close friends, colleagues, or others. What matters is that they have a way of holding you accountable to living with principles, goodness, and integrity, and you end up feeling grateful when they do.

3. Team Time: A lot of new leaders spend too much time hanging around their bosses, giving the impression they're more interested in their career climb than in developing the careers of those they're leading. Part 2 of this book is entirely devoted to leading people. For now, it's enough to know that one way to manage the perception that you're an ego-driven suck-up is to simply spend more time with the team you're leading than with your bosses.

4. Button It: If you're doing all the talking, you're not listening enough. Practice asking thoughtful questions and then pipe down and listen up. This will be hard if you're extroverted by nature. If you find yourself answering your own question, mentally recite this acronym: WAIT, which stands for why am I talking? If that doesn't work, try putting your finger over your lips. Listening connects to humility because it is a way of directing your attention to others.

5. Stay Level: Modesty involves restraint. For leaders, that means restraint from getting caught up in the belief that you are somehow "above" those you are leading. You'll get a lot of tempting cues trying to sway you in this direction. People lower on the org chart may refer to you as their "superior." You may get more expensive swag than non-leaders get. You may get to attend dinners, offsites, or boondoggles where you get pampered in ways that non-leaders don't. Don't get caught up in all that rose petal treatment. Here's an old Italian proverb worth remembering: After the game, the king and the pawn go into the same box.

6. Seek Feedback: The more you advance in the organization, the less feedback you're likely to get. Most performance evaluation processes flow downward, not upward. Be sure to occasionally ask others "How am I doing?" not out of self-consciousness or a need for false validation, but out of a genuine desire to improve. Some organizations have formal processes for providing leadership feedback, such as 360-degree feedback surveys. If your workplace has one, take advantage of it. The bigger your ego, the more honest, raw, and unfiltered feedback are likely to humble you!

7. **Consider Quitting:** Mark Costa, the CEO of Eastman Chemicals, says it right: "If you think you have all the answers, you should quit. Because you're going to be wrong." If your ego is so attached to the idea of you always having to be right, you'll save yourself a lot of disappointment by forgoing the opportunity to lead others.

8. **Count Blessings:** As you get older, you learn that shiny material things don't make you a happier person on the inside. Sometimes the opposite is true; possessions possess us. Focus on the good things you already have instead of being anxious about the grander things you haven't yet gotten. Shift to wanting what you have instead of having what you want. The quickest way to live in humble appreciation is to make a gratitude list to count your blessings.

MODERN MODESTY

There was a time when people weren't anxious for affirmation, preoccupied with the number of "likes," "thumbs-up," and emoji smiles in their comment chains. There was a time when our cameras were pointed at beautiful scenes we wanted to capture instead of our own faces. There was a time when "sharing" didn't mean posting about yourself but involved a reciprocal dialogue that welcomed others into a conversation. Those days seem long gone, replaced by a desperate need to humblebrag, virtue-signal, and take selfies with puckered lips.

The world may have become detached from the virtue of modesty, but that doesn't mean you have to. In fact, modesty can give ballast to your leadership, creating stability, strength, and steadiness. Throughout the ages, curbing the ego's insatiable appetite has been viewed as essential to mental health, moral fortitude, and self-restraint. Modesty is humility in action. It is a form of ego-taming, involving a

Leading since 2017

Kaitlin N. Giles, MS

Diversity, Equity, and Inclusion Business Partner, Southern Nuclear Company

"Don't be the smartest person in the room." This is a leadership lesson that I have to combat frequently. I have worked hard to become the "expert" in my area and am confident in my knowledge; however, from a leadership perspective, I am not doing anyone any favors by disallowing others to be the experts, too. It is important to create the space and encourage others to speak up and see themselves as experts. We want employees to feel safe and confident to be creative and willing to voice ideas.

conscious choice not to indulge your ego when it is tempting to do so. There is something attractive and admirable about a leader who justifiably could bring themselves more attention, use their power more selfishly, or take a bigger cut of the spoils...but deliberately chooses not to. People want to work with leaders who don't lose sight of their roots. People are most loyal to and comfortable around leaders who never take for granted that they were once part of the non-leader ranks. Yes, people want you to be strong and confident, but they also want you to be modest and humble. They want the focus of your leadership influence to be them, not you.

Being modest means being at ease in your own skin and knowing who you are. It means being okay toiling away in the background until the work is ready to be shown. It means asking your team for input and really valuing what they share with you. It means being comfortable with the words "I don't know" and "What do you think we should do?" It means not feeling threatened when the people you're leading start to assert their own leadership. In fact, you enjoy seeing it. It means stepping behind your team when the work you've led is being recognized. It means faithfully, strenuously, and continuously resisting the ever-present ego-temptation to make the focus of your leadership all about you.

THINK NOW/*ACT NOW*

Think Now

Describe a time when your ego got in the way too much. What did you learn from the experience that would be worth remembering as you move forward on your leadership journey?

What are some subtle ways that people have begun treating you differently or special since you've moved into your leadership role? If you let your ego get carried away with that special treatment, how might it change you? What actions can you take to ensure that you keep that special treatment in perspective?

Have you ever worked for or with someone you thought was egotistical? What did they do that makes you think of them that way? What consequences did their egotism cause? What lessons can you draw from having worked for or with them?

Which of the Ten Early Warning Signs of Ego Inflation could you check off as having had? How might you explore those signs more deeply so you experience them less frequently?

Who is a leader that you admire for their modesty and humility? What do they do that you can adopt?

Act Now

- Choose among the Eight Ways to Practice Humility offered in this chapter or pick other actions that will help you develop an ongoing practice of staying humble.
- Conduct an internet search for the word "humility" and see what you find.

- Visit the blog tab on the Giant Leap Consulting website and search for "arrogance" or "humility." We have written a lot on those topics. giantleapconsulting.com/blog/
- Do at least one specific and good thing each day for someone other than yourself.

BONUS TIP

Have you ever known someone who always seems to tell stories where they cast themselves in the central role as the hero? They'll describe how they changed someone or thing by providing some timely wisdom that only they could impart? Or, worse, they have a knack for self-righteously wagging a finger at you and saying, "Well, what you should have done was..." Don't be that person. Don't make yourself the hero of your stories. Do the opposite. Share humiliating defeats. Let people know about lessons you've learned the hard way, like the pits you've fallen in or the walls you've walked into. Tell stories about where your ego got the best of you. Better yet, if there are laughs to be had at someone's expense, let it be yours. Play the foil. Few things are as disarming and endearing as a leader who has enough humility to poke fun at him or herself.

Your two-word bonus tip is:

SHOWCASE SETBACKS

CHAPTER 6

CULTIVATE COMPOSURE

Purify Your Motives with Daily Reflection

Before we shift to part 2, which focuses on leading people, there's one final and exceptionally important self-leadership practice that will strengthen your confidence, fortify your integrity, and purify your motives. That practice is meditative reflection.

This chapter's purpose is to emphasize the importance of having a spiritual center from which your leadership operates. Don't worry, I'm not going to ask you to hold healing crystals in one hand and fire up a smudge stick in the other. Nor will you hear me tell you what to believe, or how much my faith system can beat yours in a holy rumble, or how it is heaven's favorite, or how if you don't follow the advice offered in this chapter, you'll end up under a dark sky that rains molten lava. Nope, you won't be getting a chalice full of judgment from me.

This chapter is not about the organized beliefs and practices that groups of people share as a religion. Rather, it is simply about setting aside quiet time for meditative reflection as a means of grounding, stabilizing, and centering your life and leadership. Meditative reflection is a particularly powerful practice for leaders because of its ability to subdue mental commotion and anxiety, allowing for greater personal clarity, composure, and conscientiousness.

You don't often read about spiritual fitness in secular leadership books. Maybe it's because authors are sensitive to coming off as virtue signaling. Or maybe it's because some readers view the topics as too vague or too soft or at odds with the ruthlessness that business sometimes requires. Or maybe after giving you hardscrabble leadership advice it seems a little superstitious to say, "If all else fails, pray!" My take, though, is that it is not enough to limit your leadership and personal development to just those things that strengthen or inform your thoughts and actions. Being a complete person and an effective leader requires a holistic approach that also factors in the development of your spiritual sensibilities. Your spiritual self will have a big impact on your approach to leading and on how you view and treat people.

While most leadership authors avoid the topic altogether or tiptoe around it, some notable luminaries have been quite candid about the important connection between spirituality and leadership. Dr. Stephen Covey and Ken Blanchard come to mind, the latter devoting much of his career to advancing the idea of Servant Leadership, which rejects the old school "you work for me" Machiavellian leadership attitude in favor of a more benevolent and altruistic "I serve you" approach. Similarly, Bill George, former CEO of Medtronic, management professor at Harvard University, and co-author (with Peter Sims) of *True North: Discover Your Authentic Leadership*, which emphasizes the leadership benefits of mindfulness and meditation. Likewise, popular author and vulnerability expert Brené Brown, PhD, who, in her book *Rising Strong: How the Ability to Reset Transforms the Way we Live, Love, Parent, and Lead*, writes about the importance of having daily spiritual practices.

Your spiritual self will have a big impact on your approach to leading, and on how you view and treat people.

If you cringe a little bit reading the word "spirituality," it may help to think of your spiritual self as your internal voice; the conscience that lets you know when you've done something right or when you've done something wrong. It's the inner wisdom that talks you out of doing something tempting but bad or talks you into doing something hard but good. Part of life's progression involves learning to trust this voice as it becomes more mature, insistent, and accurate. This voice will live within you for the duration of your life, right up until your last breath, so you'll do well to make friends with it and learn to heed its wise counsel!

Spirituality and leadership are both aspirational concepts, meaning there will always be a gap between who you are as a spiritual being and as a leader, and who you aim to be. On your best days, the gap should be small. You're closing the gap and being your highest spiritual self, for example, when you're acting with a high degree of self-awareness, integrity, confidence, humility, and gratitude. Those are the same indicators, of course, that you are being your best leader self. Both your spiritual self and your leader self are related to your values, ideals, conscience, and inner goodness—your integrity. Thus, your spiritual fitness is connected to how fit you are to lead.

BE QUIET

One simple way to get spiritually fit is to set aside time at the beginning of each day for contemplative silence, i.e., meditation. Starting each day with quiet reflection has a healthy centering effect. It readies you for what's to come, easing you into your day. It's restorative in that it replenishes whatever was extracted from you the day before. It lowers your stress so you can better handle the stressors you're likely to face later. It makes you more passionate about and devoted to your work. It helps reconnect you to your principles and ideals and recommits you to living with good character. Getting centered through a few minutes of peaceful prayer brings composure to your leadership, steadying your nerves so you can bring forth your best. It offers a moment of pleasant peace in a sometimes unpleasant, unpeaceful world. Certainly, this is a better way to start the day than arguing with your kids while wolfing down a microwaved breakfast burrito. Urp.

The important thing is that you learn to cultivate composure so you can view situations without the interference of your own hang-ups and insecurities and make decisions more objectively. Freeing up mental space and letting go of your anxieties, resentments, and judgments, allows you to objectively consider where and how to do better in your personal and professional life. Don't overthink it. What matters is that you set aside some quiet time at the start of each day to create some inner tranquility so you can listen to your inner voice.

Once you've quieted your mind, you start observing situations more compassionately and objectively, which helps you consider your own contribution to things that have gone wrong while helping you get clear on the actions you can take to make things right. Meditative reflection makes you thoughtful and, in my opinion, is as essential to your leadership life as mentorship, education, and experience.

LEADERSHIP BLINDNESS

Too many leaders are oblivious to themselves, operating without self-knowledge, detached from an inner value system that could otherwise ensure ethical behavior. Too many leaders reactively rush into each day, offering surface solutions to situations with complex human dynamics. Too many leaders bulldoze people and situations into submission and then act surprised when people quit or the same situations resurface again and again. The best leaders are conscientious, not oblivious. They seek a deeper level of understanding before acting or giving guidance. They've got a handle on their emotions. When things are going wrong, they spend time contemplating how their own actions may have impacted the situation and the results they're getting.

SANCTIFIED LEADERSHIP

Meditative reflection does more than bring inner peace. It is something equivalent to a human superpower. It takes every situation you're facing and harmonizes it with spiritual significance. Instead of getting frustrated, intimidated, or perplexed by a situation, you start to look for the deeper meaning or the more significant lesson the situation might be pointing to. Hassles and problems start to shift into opportunities that you can meet with your best spiritual and leader self. Situations that were once baffling start to make sense when viewed from a composed spiritual vantage point. Instead of thinking, "I am so over with Amy disrespecting my authority by disagreeing with me in meetings!" you shift to, "Why do I get so bothered when people disagree with me? How might my interactions with Amy be a good opportunity to further develop as a leader? I wonder what Amy needs? How can I help Amy?"

When you center yourself with quietness, you stop viewing situations as happening to you as some sort of cosmic punishment. Rather, situations are viewed as happening for you, to give you lessons that can make you stronger, kinder, more resilient, and generally better. Instead of feeling like a victim in a world that's constantly out to get you, you start to look forward to how events will unfold and the positive ways you might be able to influence them. You strengthen your conscious contact with your inner wisdom and innate inner goodness. Meditative reflection helps keep your motives pure, so you act in a way that's congruent with your value system.

Meditative reflection may or may not miraculously change the circumstance you're facing, but it will definitely change you and your approach. Through quiet reflection, your whole world becomes less of a hassle to be endured and a bit more of a sanctified adventure to be appreciated. The petty parts of your ego-nature start to subside, allowing you to act outside of your hang-ups or self-conscious insecurities. Situations are imbued with spiritual significance and you become more caring and compassionate in your treatment of others, giving them more of your full attention, respect, and grace. You treat people as you like to be treated, with respect and fairness. People come to treat you this way in return.

GETTING CENTERED

How you start your day will go a long way toward influencing how your day unfolds. Yes, if you've got a family, it may mean you have to get up earlier than everyone else. The payoffs, in terms of your own well-being and your treatment of others, will be worth it. Below are some ideas for cultivating composure.

Take Five: The first five minutes of your day should be centered on silence. Keep the lights dim, find a comfortable chair, place your hands on your thighs, and let your thoughts dissipate.

Heighten Senses: Tune up your senses by paying attention to what you see and hear. It's early. Maybe the sun is filling the sky with brilliant oranges and pinks against scattered gray clouds. Maybe a dog is barking in the distance. The world is waking up, and so are you.

Notice Feelings: Check in with your feelings. Are you content from having slept soundly? Or still groggy? Or anxious about an upcoming meeting? Notice your feelings, but don't attach to them. Think of them like random birds traveling along a deep blue sky. Let the birds glide through.

Directed Reading: You may find it helpful to read a paragraph or two of some calming literature or spiritual material. There are many, many books that offer daily meditations for directed contemplation.

Express Gratitude: Mentally review things going on in your life for which you are grateful. Doing so nearly always shifts one's disposition in a positive direction. Gratitude is the best antidote for negativity.

Set Intentions: Pick one positive contribution you'd like to make today. It could be a compliment you want to pay someone, or time for mentoring a direct report, or a favor you want to do for a colleague. It could also be a situation you want to deal with more maturely, courageously, and thoughtfully than you have up until now. It doesn't matter what it is, just pick one thing and commit to giving it your best.

SACRED HEARTS

Much of the leadership work I am blessed to do involves designing, developing, and delivering leadership programs for emerging leaders. Many of these programs are multi-year. During the first workshop, each participant is asked to state what they'd like the impact of their leadership to be. By far the most common response is, "I want to help others advance and grow." Even inexperienced leaders understand that impacting other human beings is the most rewarding, fulfilling, and profound responsibility about leading others.

During that first workshop, the budding leaders are also asked to share stories about a leader who impacted them and how what they learned influenced how they lead today. The stories are rich, often involving a leader who helped identify a strength or built one's confidence. Some stories are about a pivotal intercessor who caught the participant just at the moment they had started to make bad choices, and without whose influence they would have kept moving down a dark path of personal destruction.

The point is, leaders often leave an indelible imprint on people's hearts. This is a big deal! When you are in a leadership role, you will say and do things that, potentially, can forever impact the trajectory of a person's life or career. You want to make sure that, like a doctor who takes the Hippocratic Oath, at the very least, you don't harm people. Every person you encounter has a backstory. Every person has hopes and dreams in front of them. Every person has been hurt at some point in his or her life. Every person sometimes falls short and sometimes excels. Every person deserves your very best, not just because, like them, you are part of the human community but because you are a leader with unique powers of influence, the impact of which can be enduring. You'll do your best work as a leader if you treat everyone as if they were sacred and important. Because they are. Everyone.

COMPASSIONATELY TOUGH

This chapter's emphasis on quiet reflection and spiritual centeredness might confuse you into thinking that you're never supposed to get mad or confront people. Heck, even the term "Servant Leadership" sounds wimpy and servile, right? But make no mistake, I value toughness. Many of my clients are tough-as-nails construction companies based in Chicago. Plus, I'm a New Yorker. I grew up eighteen miles from the Big Apple. Watch out if you cut me off in traffic. Fuggedaboutit!

Sometimes the decisions you make or the firm feedback you give will hurt people's feelings. Oh sure, they'll go home and kick their dog and tell their spouse that you're a stink'n rat, but so what! When they deserve it, they deserve it. And sometimes they DO deserve it. What is it? Your upset, irritated, grumpy self! When should that part of you rear its ugly self? When people intentionally go behind your back, or act wholly unprofessionally with an internal or external customer, or completely ignore or intentionally defy a company value.

There will be many, many reasons that prompt and warrant your toughness along the way. So don't worry, you can be spiritually fit, compassionate, and tough. If you're spiritually strong on the inside, your motives for being tough will be in the right place. You won't be applying toughness out of jealousy, or envy, or ego, or one-upmanship. You'll be applying it to confront ethical lapses, provide strong corrective feedback, or get people to hold themselves to higher standards. Just remember, your toughness on others will have a more lasting impact if they rarely see it.

HOLY WORK

Always remember that your job as a leader is to leave people better off than you found them. Daily reflection and cultivated composure will help you rise above the muck of selfish triviality so you can meet each person and situation with a conscience that is clean and clear and ready to serve. When you get it right, every situation takes on a greater significance, every person is met with your reverence and respect and your work becomes truly sanctified. No smudge sticks required!

THINK NOW/*ACT NOW*

Think Now

Who is someone you consider to be spiritually fit? What do they do that makes them that way?

How do you typically start your day? Does your morning routine involve contemplative quiet time? If not, how might including some quiet time affect your leadership impact or approach?

How would you characterize your degree of spiritual fitness? Are you in healthy spiritual shape? If not, what commitment will you make to developing yourself along spiritual lines?

Act Now

- Read *The Seven Habits of Highly Effective People*, by Stephen R. Covey.
- Read *The Servant Leader: Transforming Your Heart, Head, Hands and Habits*, by Ken Blanchard and Phil Hodges.
- Visit the Center for Action and Contemplation at cac.org. Consider subscribing to Father Richard Rohr's weekly homily or various podcast series.

BONUS TIP

If you're a religious person, it's very likely you practice the religion you were born into through happenstance. When the only religious reference is the congregation we grew up in, our beliefs have nothing to be compared with. Void of a healthy comparison, our beliefs may harden into religious fundamentalism where we become fanatically convinced that "our way" is the "one true way." It's easy to say, "my beliefs are right, and your beliefs are wrong" if you've never been introduced to the other person's beliefs. A more authentic spiritual journey involves exploring outside of the religious traditions you grew up with so you can make informed choices about the beliefs you want to emulate, and which resonate with you most deeply. Give yourself permission to go in search of the truth, regardless of where that search may take you, even if that means venturing outside of the religious tradition you inherited through no choice of your own. There's a good chance that when you discover the truth that you're looking for, much of your inherited beliefs will be waiting there for you anyway. But so might other beliefs worth adopting and practicing.

The two-word tip is:

EXPLORE BELIEFS

Leadership Oath 1
A Promise to Be Faithful to Yourself

I promise to be a good leader of, to, and for myself. I will faithfully and regularly check-in with my own motivations, polish my conscience, and live my principles so that I can lead with goodness and pure motives.

I will be keenly aware of the privileges and advantages I have benefited from and use them to create opportunities for those who haven't enjoyed the same advantages.

I will remember the importance of personal fidelity to honor the gifts and talents with which I've been uniquely endowed.

I will be vigilant to the dangers of redlining and use my time in a disciplined and self-respectful way.

I will guard against the ever-present dangers of ego-inflation and practice the leadership essential of humility.

I will regularly make time for solitude to help center and ground myself, while purifying my motives. My leadership fitness will be built on a foundation of spiritual fitness.

I commit to leading myself with care, respect, discipline, and love.

Signed: ________________________________

Date: ________________________________

PART II

LEADING PEOPLE

The old saying is true: if you claim to be a leader and you turn around and nobody is following you, you're not a leader. You're just out for a walk.

This section focuses on one of your greatest leadership responsibilities, and the source of your most fulfilling legacy: leaving people better off than you found them. The impact you have on people can, potentially, be positive and enduring. In the same way that good leaders before you influenced who you are, the people you're now leading deserve to be enhanced by your leadership. The aim of this section is to help you make that happen by learning to foster a trustful and psychologically safe environment where people can unreservedly express and be themselves. As a new leader, you are now part of a long tradition. Leaders before you nurtured your development so you could take on greater responsibility. As they did, you developed the leader inside you. This section will help you nurture the development of the people you lead so that they too can become leaders.

CHAPTER 7

TRUST FIRST

Build Trust by First Being Trustworthy

Can I trust you? Every person you are privileged to lead needs to be able to answer that question about you affirmatively and confidently before they'll give you their best. They won't be able to answer that question instantly as they'll form their answer based on your actions, the environment you foster, and your treatment of each team member. They will need to settle the question before they fully believe you are on their side. So, are you trustworthy?

Trust is a complex and very personal subject, impacted by such things as the stability of your upbringing, your perception of your self-worth, your personal disposition and how open to scrutinizing it is, and the degree to which you have suffered through betrayals and violations in your life. All of this has impacted you even before you must take into consideration the people with whom you hope to build trust and whether you can trust each of them.

All of us seem to exist on a grand continuum that ranges from extreme naiveté to extreme self-protection. Ignorance resides at either end. It is being open to the point of trusting those who are bound to take advantage of our trust, but it's also being so untrusting that we are unable to develop any relationships. Both ends are dangerous to you or to others. Whatever your background and wherever you reside on the continuum, as a leader you have to find a way to trust those you're responsible for leading or you will fail. Trust is elemental to developing the strong interpersonal bonds that underpin healthy relationships between leaders and those they're leading.

There's a reason this book's first part was dedicated to you Leading Yourself. Before others can find you trustworthy, you must fully trust yourself. All that inner work suggested in the early chapters is to help you get right with yourself, so that you can consistently trust yourself to do the right thing as you understand the right thing to be. The essential inner work associated with Leading Yourself is about purifying your motives to help you rise above the incessant pull of your base nature. To fully trust yourself, you'll need to continually monitor and, if necessary, purify your motives. It's not about second-guessing yourself and being self-conscious, it's about your leadership fitness. When you know in your core that you can trust yourself and that you are worthy of the trust of others, your leadership fitness will be much stronger.

Leading since **1996**

Mariana Tejera

West Region Sales Director, IES Communications

A lot of leaders place the highest importance on bringing in big sales at high margins and growing revenue. Yes, those things are important. That said, if you're able to develop and capitalize on each team member's strengths, jointly establish challenging goals, and create a harmonious and trustful environment, you'll do so well with customers that the revenue will have no choice but to flow.

MAINTAIN TRUSTWORTHINESS

Which is more difficult for you: trusting yourself or trusting others? If you're like most people, trusting others is more challenging. Surprisingly, when my company asks this question on anonymous leadership surveys, there is always a small percentage (generally about 10 percent) who say that trusting themselves is more difficult. I used to scratch my head about this until I was soliciting answers to this question during a presentation given to about one hundred healthcare workers. I said, "There's always a number of people who have difficulty trusting themselves. I wonder if there is someone here who could shed some light on that answer for the ninety percent of folks who have more difficulty trusting others?"

Slowly, a woman in the back of the room raised her hand. "I can only speak for myself, but four years ago I went into treatment for substance abuse. For years I had struggled with addiction, often promising myself that things would be different this time, and then I'd relapse. Today, I trust myself... but just for today. If I project out to tomorrow, all bets are off. Treatment, and the twelve-step program I'm in today, helped me stay focused on today."

You can imagine the courage it took for her to reveal herself that way. In about thirty seconds, she had illuminated, starkly and viscerally, why someone might not trust themselves. Her words also gave people permission to consider if their own histories might include stories where they did something to let themselves down, to betray self-trust. Who among us hasn't, at one time or another, rejected who we are by pretending to be someone we aren't? Who hasn't made a resolution or commitment, only to break it when it got tested? Who hasn't bitten their tongue and swallowed a deeply held belief for fear of offending others who believed otherwise? All of us have given ourselves reasons not to trust ourselves. To be an effective leader and one people want to work for, you must be trustworthy. And trustworthiness is a temporary condition that needs continual maintenance.

When you know, in your core, that you trust yourself and that others can trust you, your fitness to lead will be much stronger.

CONNECTED HEARTS

I once knew a business owner who would sneak out of the office whenever he went on vacation. He would arrange his desk to suggest that he had just stepped away to the restroom, first filling up a steaming cup of coffee and putting it on a coaster next to an unfinished note. He'd exit the backdoor when nobody was looking, where his wife would be waiting with their car to head to the airport. He believed that as soon as people knew he was gone from the office, they'd start to ease up and goof off. In his mind, they could only be trusted to do work when he was there to watch them doing it. He distrusted his workforce so much that he met it with his own deceit. As witnesses to his childish behavior, how much do you think his workforce trusted him? Zilch.

Some leaders give off vibes that make everyone around them uneasy. If you've ever worked with an uptight, short-fused, purse-lipped, perpetually angry feudal lord, you know what I mean. They aren't really leaders. They're rulers, and they're bent on continually reminding you that they're the boss and they don't trust you. What do rulers like that get in return? Direct reports who are fearful, tepid, subservient, resentful, and disloyal. Don't be a ruler.

Human beings have a way of getting jaded over time. We

suffer through a few betrayals and start building walls around our hearts. It's a way of protecting ourselves from future hurts. With our prickliness, we keep people from drawing too close. This distance, which we've created, ensures that we won't be taken advantage of in the way that sometimes happens when you care too much and then are betrayed. This is a form of self-protection through trust rejection. By rejecting trust and the risks it comes with, we live only out of our heads, devoid of compassion, irrationally over-rational. We come to trust only things that can be verified, proven, predicted, and controlled. People rarely count among those things.

The dangers of living in a hyper-rationalistic, overly self-protective, and non-trusting way are well known. My favorite illustration of this is a sculpture by the French artist Auguste Rodin. This statue was the result of a commission Rodin was given early in his career to build a monumental gate for a decorative arts museum being built in Paris. The terms of the commission dictated that the gate be decorated with images inspired by Dante's Inferno. Rodin decided to go beyond the commission's terms and create a statue that depicted the torment and suffering of humanity itself. He worked on the piece for over ten years, never fully satisfied, and kept adding new images. In the process, the statue became a sort of laboratory where Rodin created small versions of figures and images that would eventually find their way into later pieces, and a few became famous as singular works of art. In fact, sitting above the gate's entrance is the figure that eventually became the artist's most famous sculpture: *The Thinker*.

Rodin's decision to situate *The Thinker* above the gate's entrance could not have been coincidental. It suggests that Rodin, like so many sages before him, knew that a life that subjects each experience to the brain's investigation, evaluation, and dispassionate objectification is no life at all. Heads and hearts aren't supposed to be disconnected from each other. Our heads keep us from making decisions out of impulse or infatuation. Our hearts keep our heads from making us impersonal robots. The connection is important. When we trust only our rational mind, we miss out on the rich returns possible from taking chances on others when we follow our hearts. Rodin's sculpture suggests that what ultimately awaits the person who lives only rationally, directed by his head and disconnected from his heart, is unending misery. Fittingly, Rodin titled this work *The Gates of Hell*.

DISTRUSTFUL VIBES

The vibe you give off to others will tell them whether to trust you. Use the checklist below to gauge whether people trust you, and if not, where you might have some work to do. A leader who isn't worthy of people's trust...

- Always trusts his or her own instincts above those of others.
- Intentionally assigns goals they know are unreachable, believing that people will at least improve a little by stretching toward the impossible.
- Tasks people with mundane jobs just to keep them busy because it "builds character."
- Gives him or herself a pass before ever apologizing or admitting a mistake.
- Punishes even honest mistakes harshly, to prevent future mistakes.
- Doesn't smile, maintaining a resting poker face for fear of revealing true emotions.
- Has no backbone when dealing with their own bosses and higher-ups.
- Spins messages and shades the truth in whatever ways serves his or her purposes.
- Enables backchanneling so that individual team members can

come to him or her, dishing about their teammates behind each other's backs.

- Likes to be unpredictable to keep people on their toes.

Seems like a draconian way to lead, right? Yet here we are in the modern age with so many leaders still relying on Byzantine leadership approaches. Leaders like this don't deserve trust, mostly because, to them, people are objects to be manipulated and exploited and are unworthy of dignity, respect, and development.

DISARM YOURSELF

Some leaders prefer keeping their direct reports "on their toes" by making them worry. The idea seems to be that if the leader can keep his or her directs in a perpetual state of anxiety, the leader can rest assured that people will remain conscientious about the task at hand. Some worrying, they reason, is good. So they inject a little fear while assigning tasks, placing extra emphasis on the consequences of doing a bad or subpar job on the task. They amp up the fear by harping on the risks and punishments of getting the task wrong, versus painting a vision of how to get the task done right. Usually, the fear-stoking comes with an exclamation point in the form of the words, "...or else!"

There will be times when you too will be tempted to equate worry with conscientiousness, particularly when assigning consequential tasks. It's a strange strategy, but one not uncommon among new leaders, the idea that you'll be able to worry less if you can just make them worry more. And making them hyper-afraid of the consequences is the cheap way to do that. It's not much different from parents trying to get their kids to be good by scaring them. "Stop that ruckus or Santa will put coal in your stocking!"

News flash for new leaders: adults don't need threats to do a good job! If you set the conditions for high performance by clearly explaining the standards expected for each task, by involving your directs in shaping how those tasks will be done, and by being readily available to support them throughout the process, they'll "own" their work with a high degree of conscientiousness. They'll also respect and trust you more than if you're a worry-stoking fearmonger.

Gary Peck, a Chicago-based executive coach for whom I have enormous respect, says, "Before you become a leader, sometimes you have conversations around the lunchroom table about your boss. When you become a leader, you become the subject of those lunchroom conversations!" He goes on to explain, "Everything you say and do sets an example. The 'how' starts to matter as much as the 'what.' Meaning, when you move into a leadership role, your tone, composure, and level-headedness will matter just as much—and perhaps more—than the actual content of your directives or guidance."

I'm guessing you don't want your direct reports to be uneasy around you. In fact, you should want the opposite, for your directs to be comfortable in your presence. Not barefeet-on-your-desk comfortable—it's still work and you're still in a role that should carry some deference—but comfortable

Leading since **1991**

Gary Peck
President, GWP Consulting, and Coaching since 2003

Let's also remember that everything you don't say and do also sends a message to your people. Non-actions, such as not confronting poor performance, avoiding hard conversations, and not intervening when you should, convey a lot about you as a leader. It's hard to be respected when you don't handle what needs to be handled.

enough to share honest opinions, challenge assumptions, and express counterviewpoints...without fear. As Gary Peck suggests, your own demeanor will have a great influence over the degree to which your directs will be comfortable around you. And how you carry yourself during interactions with them will determine whether their lunchroom conversations about you are glowing or glowering.

TRUST COURAGE

Trust takes courage. No amount of upfront scrutinizing and evaluation will entirely remove the risks that come with trusting others. So, if you're an "I'll trust you when you prove you can be trusted" kind of person, you need to get over that. There will never be enough proof to fully remove all the risks. There will always be a chance that you will trust someone and they'll let you down. Even our deepest and most valued relationships are subject to that constant risk, although likely to a lesser extent as time goes on.

Rather than trying to insulate yourself from harm, I invite you to view trust as something that requires courage. It takes courage to trust others because it means accepting the risk that they could let you down. For some leaders, trusting others will take little courage, for others a tremendous amount. Regardless, in either case the dangers of not assuming the risk of trusting others is more harmful. As a leader, if you can't muster the courage to trust, you'll be swamped doing tasks you've outgrown, stunt people's development, and have poor and shallow relationships. The choice of whether to summon the courage to trust others really comes down to whether you would rather trust others and assume the risk of being let down or not trust others and live in a constant state of suspicion and paranoia?

Leading since 1989

Brian Mazzei

Chief Operating Officer, Aldridge Electric Incorporated

The biggest failures are when leaders or team leads dictate their plan and drop the mic. You need to continually check in with your team and give them support throughout the work getting done. In addition to helping the work get done, you checking in helps you monitor progress. Trust but verify.

In my company's courage-building workshops we look at three different behavioral buckets of courage: the courage to try new things (TRY Courage), the courage to be a truth-teller (TELL Courage), and the courage to trust others (TRUST Courage). TRUST Courage is described as the courage it takes to get disarmed and form strong interpersonal relationships. It's not the kind of strong bravery that one typically associates with the word "courage." Rather, it involves emotional vulnerability, such as it takes to...

- genuinely care about the concerns and interests of others.
- take suggestions and go along with ideas that are not your own.
- feel joy and not envy when others are successful, and generously express gratitude.
- delegate substantial tasks with support, and not micromanage.
- openly share some of your personal, nonwork identity.
- willingly accept help and support when offered.
- be open to candid and constructive feedback about your leadership style and approach.

Some people, men in particular, don't traditionally view "vulnerability" as strength. But strength is exactly what it is. Strength of character. And when others see you apply your courage in this way, not only will they come to trust you more but they'll also feel empowered to safely be vulnerable too. There's a certain give-to-get at play; when you trust others, others come to trust you. Rather than wait for those around you to prove their trustworthiness, start by summoning your own courage and be the first to step off the high dive. Lead the way. Trust First.

CARE MORE

Years ago, a few years after starting my company, I was having a performance review with one of my employees. After reviewing his good work and pointing out some improvement opportunities, I asked him if there was anything I could do to be a better leader for him. After a few beats of silence, he said, "Yes, there is. Let me pose the request in the form of a question: What are the names of my two kids?"

I didn't know.

I was thoroughly ashamed, as I should have been. The employee had shared scores of stories about his two children, Alicia and Kellen, but I had never bothered to learn their names. Until that moment, when he would tell me stories, I'd make believe I was listening while I was really just waiting to talk. My mind was rarely on the story he was telling me. It was usually on the next task that he or I needed to get done.

That painfully embarrassing episode taught me the importance of genuinely valuing the people you work with by simply paying attention to them when they talk to you. What did my colleague want of me as a leader? Two words: just listen!

ENTRUSTING OTHERS

One leadership luminary whom I've long admired is Ken Blanchard, the author or co-author of over sixty books, including the classic, *The One Minute Manager,* co-authored with Spencer Johnson. Dr. Blanchard and I are both members of ISA, an association of organizational development and instructional design companies. Each year members of ISA gather for a business retreat to continue to grow and develop ourselves so that we can all better serve our clients. While at the retreat one evening, I arrived late for dinner and sat down by myself at a table in the far back of the conference room. All the other tables had been taken up, which turned out to be my good fortune. Soon after I sat down, Ken and his wife Margie walked in and sat down at my table. I was kind of nervous because, as a leadership development practitioner, I was very familiar with Dr. Blanchard's books and research on leadership. I had been introduced to his Situational Leadership Model, developed with Dr. Paul Hersey, in graduate school over thirty years ago. His influence in the field spanned decades before that. Yet here he was in the flesh, a giant in the field of leadership development, sitting right next to me.

Figuring I'd better take advantage of the opportunity, I asked Dr. Blanchard if he could sum up much of his work with one key leadership lesson, what would it be? He smiled and said, "Great leaders take the time to build trust with the people they lead. Investing the time to build trust with people is what separates average leaders from great ones. The amazing thing is how little time it takes to build that trust."

Dr. Blanchard went on to explain that if a leader simply invests fifteen minutes of quality time every week or two by building trust with direct reports, everything is transformed. The key is what happens in those fifteen minutes. It can't be about having the person report their status on assignments or what the person is doing to advance the leader's agenda. No, those fifteen minutes must be solely focused on the human being—not the "worker"—in front of them. How are they doing? How's life? What is important to them right now? How are things going in their career? Is there any support they need from me or anything they feel I should know so I can be a better leader for them? Fifteen minutes devoted just to them.

Dr. Blanchard has written a lot about Servant Leadership—the idea that leaders serve those they lead, not the other way around. The leader is there to provide access to resources, remove roadblocks, and provide an environment where everyone can do great work. The leader serves the team. That means dedicating time to each individual team member. The fifteen minutes Dr. Blanchard suggests is about getting to know each individual team member and building trust with them. Doing so gives you a keen understanding of what they hope to achieve with their career, what their priorities and goals are, and what drives and motivates them. Knowing these things will help you be a better leader for them because you'll have a much clearer picture of how to best serve them.

As if to punctuate the point, Dr. Blanchard added, "Any leader who says they can't find fifteen minutes a week for a direct report is full of baloney!"

THINK NOW/*ACT NOW*

Think Now

Are you trustworthy? Elaborate on your answer.

What experiences have you had that might be impacting how you approach trust today?

As a leader, what do you view as the risks associated with trusting your direct reports? What are the risks associated with not trusting them?

Which of the Distrustful Vibes might you be giving off? How might it be impacting your relationships with your direct reports?

What are a few actions you could take to be more vulnerable and demonstrate Trust Courage?

Act Now

- Identify the current criteria you use for trusting others by completing this statement: "I will trust you when..." Evaluate the list. Which criteria might no longer be relevant or might be counterproductive to the goal of trusting others?
- In a disarmed moment, such as over lunch, have a conversation with your team about what role trust currently plays on the team, and should play on the team. Converse about ways to improve the level of team trust, if needed.
- After discussing trust with the team, get a piece of flipchart paper and divide it in half. Label the left side "Busters" and the right side "Builders." Working with the team, identify actions/behaviors that "bust" trust, and those that "build" it.
- Take a greater interest in the topic of workplace trust. Pick up a trust-related book by any one of these authors: Drs. Dennis and Michelle Reina, Stephen M.R. Covey, and David Horsager.
- Schedule individual fifteen-minute check-in meetings with each direct report. Decide with them how frequently you'll meet for future check-ins. I recommend at least every two weeks.

BONUS TIP

Have you ever worked for a boss who used their moodiness as part of their management style? Maybe they would sigh loudly with frustration, or shake their head in disgust, or roll their eyes, conveying how ridiculous they thought an idea was, or fold their arms and cock their heads to the side as if they were thinking, "Really?!" They use their moods to treat others like errant children.

Being a leader doesn't make you someone's parent. Your direct reports aren't your children, and they deserve to be treated like the adults they are. Trying to change people's behaviors through your moods is patronizing and immature.

Your two-word bonus tip is, don't subject people to your

MOOD MANAGEMENT

CHAPTER 8

CREATE SAFETY

Promote Courage with Psychological Safety

If you had to choose between employees who comfortably played it safe and those who consistently acted with courage, who would you rather have reporting to you? The answer should be easy and obvious: you'd rather have courageous employees. However, in times of change and uncertainty, you'll find that it's common for people to hunker down and seek safety as they take stock of the shifting terrain. It's also common during unstable times for fear to direct their behavior. They become distracted, suspicious, and unproductive. Here's the rub: in today's work world, change, uncertainty, and instability are constants. Meaning, a lot of workers are in a constant state of fear and safety-seeking. Dangerously so.

Fear is bad for business. It lowers morale, loyalty, and retention. If you could calculate the Total Cost of Fear (TCF) in the workplace, it would be enormous. When employees are afraid, they're not fully productive. They spend an inordinate amount of time speculating about their fate rather than advancing goals. They are prone to hiding mistakes for fear of harsh consequences. They stifle bad news, keeping you and other leaders oblivious to dangers and risks that would otherwise be dealt with. They often "check out," physically present but mentally disengaged. They withhold innovative ideas, opting instead for safe choices. Many fearful employees will leave just as soon as they find a safer harbor where they can apply their full creative selves. Despite these common impacts of a fear-based workplace, a lot of leaders still use fear-stoking as the primary means of motivating employees to get things done. You can't be one of those leaders. They've done too much damage already.

Your aim should be to inspire courageous behavior among those you are leading. Courage is the antidote to fear and safety-seeking. Courage causes people to show initiative and "step up to the plate," speak with assertiveness and honesty, and embrace the uncertainties that accompany change. Courage gives people the backbone to face fierce challenges, stretch toward higher levels of performance, and move outside their safe comfort zone in pursuit of improvement. Where fearful workers are safety-seekers, courageous workers are opportunity-seekers, and your success as a leader will be directly related to your ability to counteract the negative impacts of fear by activating people's courage.

Ironically, the most effective way to get people to stop seeking safety is to create safety! You foster an environment that is safe enough to promote risk. The safer the environment you create, the more willing people will be to take risks. Thus, if you want people to be fully engaged and accountable, take on greater responsibility and harder assignments, unreservedly assert creative ideas, and generally be more leaderlike themselves, you have to make it safe to do so. You must create safety.

ENCOURAGE COURAGE

Years ago I had two bosses with distinctly different dispositions. I directly reported to one of the bosses and "dotted-lined" to the other. Both were responsible for providing input to my performance review; thus, both could impact my career. The boss to whom I indirectly reported to was uptight and outwardly transmitted anxiety. She was hyper-focused on risks that needed to be avoided. She would assign me a "problem" and emphasize all the bad things that would happen if I screwed up. She lit me up with fear, pointing out all the ways the assignment could fail, and how if it did, it would reflect poorly on her and the company and would torpedo my career. "Let me be clear," she'd say, "this is your problem now. Solve it...or else!"

What was going on? Her own fear was spilling over to me. Her real concern was that if I botched the assignment, it would reflect on her judgment to task me with it in the first place. Injecting me full of fear was a sort of insurance policy. She must have thought that the more afraid I was, the more consumed I would be with doing a good job, reducing the chance of her getting blamed for my doing the job badly. It may be twisted logic, but it's all too common.

The boss I directly reported to was older and far more composed. He would assign me similar tasks but never called them "problems." He'd say, "There's a lot of opportunity in this assignment." Then he'd ask me for my initial ideas for getting the job done successfully before adding a few of his own. He'd focus on the positive difference the task could have on our client, and how a good job could lead to the client trusting us with even bigger assignments. Then he'd say something like, "I'm confident that you'll do a great job, and I'm here to support you in any way that you need. That's my job. So please tap into me as a resource as you move forward. Let's get something on the calendar early next week to catch up."

A lot of leaders focus more on the conditions that they don't want than the ones they do. In my book *Courage Goes to Work*, I call this en*fear*ing people, because it's the opposite of encouraging them. These fear-transmitting leaders will say,

"Whatever you do, don't drop that ball!"—which gets your brain thinking about dropped balls. Other leaders, like my direct boss, shift your focus to all the things you can do to keep the balls in the air. They encourage you by focusing on the opportunities that a good job will garner, versus the ugly consequences of failure. It's not that they avoid risk; they just make it safer to take risks by not letting it freak them (or you) out.

Much of the first part of this book dealt with getting you right with yourself. Your own emotional composure, or lack thereof, will make a big impact on those around you. If you're overly critical or short-tempered, or if you freak out in the face of challenge, that behavioral junk will be transmitted to the people you lead, potentially creating an emotional contagion where fear permeates the work environment and people become tentative and hesitant. They start to play it too safe. If, on the other hand, you know who you are, you're comfortable in your own skin and are skilled at modulating and taming your own stress, the atmosphere you'll create at work will be far more enjoyable, productive, innovative, and actually safe.

TELL COURAGE

In chapter 7, I offered three different behavioral expressions of courage. I emphasized the importance of TRUST Courage—the courage of vulnerability. This chapter emphasizes TELL Courage—the courage it takes to speak candidly and assertively.

TELL Courage is the behavioral expression that people commonly refer to when asked for examples of courageous behavior that they have seen at work. Most often, people cite examples of the reticent person who, voice shaking, spoke up for everyone in the room and confronted their leadership about something everyone but the leaders was experiencing. TELL Courage is important because, without it, people will avoid the necessary confrontations that fortify healthy relationships and teams.

TELL Courage is at work anytime you give direct feedback to a direct report, peer, or boss to support their growth, or to hold them accountable to agreed-upon goals and values. It's there when teammates vigorously disagree with one another to produce better outcomes or decisions. It's working when lower-level employees stop production because specs aren't being properly followed or safety is threatened. And it's there when you level with people about company moves that will negatively impact them. TELL Courage is all about touchstone honesty, and it's essential to sound leadership. It's also hard because people generally avoid hurting other people's feelings, and, yes, sometimes the truth does indeed hurt.

Here are a few quick tips for applying TELL Courage:

Flag It: When you have to say something that will require your courage, underscore its importance by saying, "There's something important I'd like to discuss with you."

Be Precise: Know exactly the message you want to convey, and the purpose for conveying it. Craft your message with precision. Don't wing it.

Anticipate Responses: Identify the ideal response you'd like your message to receive, and the response you realistically think it will receive. Figure out adjustments you may need to make to your message depending on the response you get.

Buddy Test: If it's a sensitive message, consider practicing the conversation with someone you trust and who works outside of your organization.

Compliment Too: Don't restrict TELL Courage to just communicating hard truths. Also, use it when you notice people giving an exceptional effort or being a good sport or living the organization's values. Use Tell Courage to give generous and sincere praise.

Remember, no leader in your organization's most senior ranks got there by avoiding saying bold things.

PURPOSEFUL DISSENT

It takes a lot of inner strength and personal confidence to not view a challenge to your ideas as a challenge to your authority. A lot of leaders confuse the two, getting rankled when someone points out flaws in their thinking. Good ideas are durable, though, and can withstand scrutiny, disagreement, and challenge. In fact, good decisions require those things. Rather than get defensive or view challenges to your ideas as undermining your authority, you'd do better to create an environment that invites those challenges.

McKinsey and Company is highly regarded as one of the world's premier strategy consulting firms. To give its clients exceptional guidance, the company itself and the consultants who work there must maintain what it calls an "independent perspective" while upholding the highest professional standards.

One of the ways the company fosters independent perspectives is to create an environment where its consultants are encouraged to strongly advocate for what they believe to be true. The way to have a successful career at McKinsey is to be fully engaged, which includes offering thoughts and ideas that may run counter to the prevailing thoughts and ideas of others, such as peers, bosses, or clients. In other words, to provide exceptional guidance, you are obliged to rigorously test and challenge each other's assumptions, biases, and logic. McKinsey refers to this as the "obligation to engage and dissent."

It is the duty of every consultant, regardless of rank, to dissent when they can substantiate their thoughts with a clear and compelling rationale. The most junior person in the room is free to openly disagree with the most senior person. McKinsey views this freedom as one of its most important controls on quality. What matters is producing ideas and decisions that are robust, vetted, and well-tested, not affirming the boss's rank or ego.

INVITE CHALLENGE

Some leaders, in particular new ones, get a little too attached to having their "authority" respected. Often, it's a vestige of one's upbringing, where one of your earliest lessons is to respect authority figures, be it your parents, elders, clergy, or law enforcement. Now that you are the authority figure, you may become sensitive to the kind of disagreement that your parents would have viewed as "back talk" and would have sternly addressed when you were a child. But you're not leading children. You don't get to ground them or send them to their room without dinner. You're leading adults who deserve to be treated as such. Were they to pleasantly agree with your every thought and preference it would be a serious danger to your leadership. Expecting childish subservience also robs them of the chance to build upon, improve, or enhance innovative ideas. You'll often find that they'll make your ideas better.

The kind of safety I'm referring to in this chapter is what organizational psychologists and consultants now call psychological safety. It's a topic that is getting a lot of attention and proving to be a key differentiator for leaders and teams that perform at a superior level. One hallmark of a psychologically safe environment is that people can openly challenge each other's ideas or assumptions without fear of being punished. As it relates to leadership, this means people need to be able to challenge your ideas and assumptions. Clearly, being able to openly challenge each other's ideas shouldn't give people permission to be malcontent misanthropes. Who wants to work on a team where you can't say a single thing without it being subject to the scrutiny and objection of others? No team benefits from intellectual knife fights. Instead, work with a team to establish boundaries to guide constructive challenging of ideas, such as...

- Never be intentionally hurtful. Be helpful.
- Value team relationships and great ideas above individual egos.
- Honesty delivered with brutality is unhelpful.
- Diplomacy that waters down messages is unhelpful.
- How you say it matters as much as what you say.
- Make sure you fully understand the other person's point of view.
- Strive for unity and alignment, not sameness and conformity.
- Be responsible for your own emotions.
- When you're wrong, own it like an adult.
- When you're right, stay compassionate. Don't gloat.

Establishing protocols for constructive dissent prevents team members from suffering in silence, either because they don't feel safe challenging the ideas and assumptions of others, or because they've been the recipient of harsh blowback when doing so. Steven Wolff, an expert on team emotional intelligence and the developer of the Inspired Teams survey, suggests that team members be given the freedom to govern themselves by calling out when inconsistencies develop between the team's values and how it is really operating. It can be as simple as inspiring a healthy team-improvement conversation by giving everyone permission to say, "Hey team, I'm noticing [state the inconsistency]. What's up with that? Are others noticing this too?"

STAY COMPOSED

The leaders we admire most are those who remain composed when the potential for anxiety is high. As you progress in your career, you'll face all sorts of challenging people and situations that will tempt you into crappy behavior quite unbefitting a leader. A tremendous amount of your ability to influence others—what leadership is all about—will come down to your personhood. People should come away from interactions with you feeling more confident and positive about the task at hand and themselves. Thus, not freaking out when your buttons get pushed is a critical leadership skill. Here are some ways to stay composed:

Observe Yourself: Especially when you notice yourself getting triggered, make a habit of asking yourself, "What's going on with me?" Watch what's happening in and around you without judgment or attachment, as if it were happening to someone else.

Claim Emotions: As you observe yourself, claim the emotion you're experiencing. Think, "I can tell [insert the emotion] is influencing me." Notice you're not identifying with the emotion. You're not saying, "I am angry." Rather, you are experiencing anger. Emotions are always shifting, changing, and flushing through you, so you are never a stationary emotion.

Peacefully Pause: It's never a good idea to converse, decide, or act while your emotional innards are rattling. It helps to grab a quick moment to settle yourself. Even calling for a five- or ten-minute break so you can take a few deep breaths and gain some perspective will help you reclaim your composure. The more rattled you are, the bigger the pause you may need.

Uplevel Yourself: Once you've reclaimed your composure, consider how your leadership can best serve the person or situation you're engaging with. As a leader, you should uphold and emulate the behavioral standards you'd like others to stand up for. After you've recomposed, think, "What can I do to be a good leader at this moment?"

When emotional storm clouds pay you a visit, it helps to remember that you are not the clouds. Clouds will come and go, traveling through you, sometimes with rain, sometimes with lightning. But they will always lift eventually, revealing a royal blue sky. That blue sky is you, as your best and most composed leader self.

PROVIDE SUPPORT

In psychologically safe work environments, people are more willing to ask for help. Generally, asking for help is a hard thing to do. Employers expect a certain degree of self-sufficiency; they want you to be able to solve a lot of challenges yourself. There's always a danger that the person who asks for help will be seen as somehow weak, needy, or incompetent. But it's far more dangerous to have overburdened employees missing deadlines and causing project delays. As a leader, you want to promote an environment where asking for help is seen as smart, responsible, and expected. The support you provide when people ask for help is one of the most effective ways of promoting that environment.

Remember the axiom, "No surprises!" mentioned at the start of the book? It connects directly to the willingness to ask for help. Surprises, in the form of project or customer disasters, result when people try to handle adverse situations by themselves, often hiding the situation from their leaders until it starts to blow up. Leaders get especially frustrated when disasters could have been prevented if they'd merely been made aware of the situation much earlier in the process. To promote this, and to destigmatize the potential negative reactions to asking for "help," one of my clients launched the Boost program. When early red flags are identified on a project, often by the project leader, a small Boost team—comprising the project leader's boss and their boss's boss, the company CFO, and other leaders as required—is quickly mobilized to identify the root causes of the red flags, develop and assign mitigating actions, provide training to develop impactful solutions, and schedule follow-up Boost sessions until the project issues have been resolved. It's an all-hands-on-deck approach that is designed to boost the project and its leader by giving positive and tangible project support, not punishment and embarrassment.

As a new leader, you may find that the issues and challenges that team members bring you may not warrant such a full-throttle approach as the Boost program. Nonetheless, the support you provide people who ask for help needs to be practical, useful, and positive. Otherwise, they'll stop asking for your help. The help you provide may come in the form of additional resources and training or just more of your focused attention. What matters is viewing it as a positive thing when people have the courage to ask for help and responding with a positive boost of your own.

COMMUNICATE AUTHENTICALLY

When you move into a leadership role, your words often take on greater significance. A passing reference about the lousy meeting snacks may be construed as a directive for someone to bring fruit to future meetings. You may transmit your annoyances or frustrations at decibel three, but some team members will receive them at decibel five and communicate them to others at a more urgent decibel eight. This is sometimes referred to as the Megaphone Effect. Because a leader's words carry more weight, you've got to be thoughtful about what and how you communicate.

People feel safest around things that are real and true, whether those things are objects or people; we don't like fakes. Most people seem to be equipped with an authenticity detector, and we can easily tell when we're being placated, patronized, or in some other way manipulated. As a leader, you've got to pay close attention to the words you use and the messages you send, but not in a way that ends up making you sound stilted or plastic. People want to know that you are reasonable and real. That you can be reached and reasoned with and that you won't use your role as an artificial barrier between you and them.

In my company's leadership programs, we spend a lot of time helping leaders adopt "Leader Language"—language that invites people's receptiveness instead of defensiveness. Usually, small word changes make a big difference. For example, depending on how you ask it, the words "Why did you do that?" can be viewed as accusatory and interrogative, prompting defensiveness. But a simple word shift to "Help me understand how you came to choose that option" invites understanding and openness. Of course, words are only part of the communication equation. The other part is your intonation. You can literally change the entire meaning of a sentence simply by where you put the emphasis. Here's a quick example. Read the following sentence multiple times, each time emphasizing a different word.

I didn't say you had an attitude problem.

See what I mean? If you say, "***I*** didn't say you had an attitude problem," it implies someone else did. If you say, "I didn't say you had ***an*** attitude problem," it suggests they had far more problems than that! You get the idea. Here are some other simple shifts (see Table 1) that will make it safer for people to put down their defenses...

Communicating thoughtfully and respectfully is how you'll come to connect with the team and each team member. That connection is made up of things like goodwill, loyalty, and kinship. You want your conversations to enrich and deepen that connection because it reflects the strength of your team bond. Some leaders, unfortunately, use language to win, as if every conversation were a competition that they

Defensive Language	Receptive Language
"That idea wasn't bad."	"That idea was good."
"Here's what you need to do..."	"What do you think needs to be done?"
"Why are you getting so upset!?"	"You seem to feel strongly about this."
"You are wrong."	"I see it differently."
"You make me so frustrated!"	"I'm feeling frustrated."
"You always..." or "You never..."	"This happens relatively frequently." or "This needs to happen more."
"You aren't being very clear."	"I don't understand. Can you say it differently?"
"That's a foolish thing to say."	"That's disappointing to hear. Can you reframe what you said?"
"You keep repeating yourself. Move on!"	"I've heard you mention this before. Is there something you feel you haven't been able to express?"
"If I were you, I'd..."	"I'm happy to share some thoughts if you think that would be helpful."
"You need to stop doing X."	"I encourage you to consider Y."

Table 1. Defensive language vs. Receptive language.

must dominate. You'll do better to view your conversations as a chance to collaborate and co-create with your team, versus trouncing them with your debate skills.

CONFRONT SOBERLY

When you've contributed to establishing a psychologically safe work environment, people will be able to confront and challenge each other more frequently and respectfully. That doesn't mean there won't be lapses in judgment and/or issues related to poor performance. There will be. And if you give people a pass, you will undermine the very safety you sought to build. The whole point of creating a psychologically safe workplace is to allow people to take risks with one another. When you as a leader can't muster the courage to confront performance issues, you're letting fear dictate your behaviors. You're also losing a ton of credibility with your team. Your team needs to know you'll soberly address, and actively work to resolve, breaches of conduct. Here are a few things you absolutely have to confront when you're the leader:

- ethical violations
- sexual harassment (consult your boss, and legal and HR teams and take corrective action...fast!)
- racism (consult your boss, and legal and HR teams and take corrective action...fast!)
- lapses in safety and quality protocols (consult your boss and the safety or quality director)
- drug or alcohol use at work (consult your boss, safety director, and Employee Assistance Program [EAP] professionals [if your company has an EAP program])
- unprofessional behavior
- costly or repeat mistakes
- bad-mouthing teammates, customers, or anybody else

People want and expect you to confront others as part of your leadership role. They just want you to do so in a respectful and straightforward way. Nobody needs to get their face smooshed in their own mistake like an errant dog. Breaches of conduct, fortunately, are rare. Even when they happen, most, thankfully, won't involve sexual harassment, racism, or ethical breaches—which warrant much more intense involvement on your part, and severe consequences from your organization. For more straightforward breaches, your team just wants you to have a serious but private conversation that helps the person acknowledge what happened, fully commit themselves to fix the situation, and ensure that it won't happen again. Standards of conduct are important and upholding them is a central expectation your team has of you. Knowing that you will swiftly confront breaches of conduct helps keep the work environment safe for everyone. Use your TELL Courage!

THINK NOW/*ACT NOW*

Think Now

Have you ever worked in an environment that was characterized by a lot of fear? How did the leaders contribute to this environment? What were the consequences? How did it affect you personally?

Have you ever used fear to motivate people to start or stop doing something? How did the fear impact the results you did or didn't achieve? How did the fear impact your relationship with the people you were enfearing?

What are some techniques you already use when you lose your composure and attempt to reclaim it? Which technique works the best?

Generally, how do you react to being challenged? How might you act better or differently?

What are some helpful phrases that you've heard other leaders use, or that you have used, to successfully disarm people so they can safely open up?

Act Now

- During lunch or in an informal team meeting, have the team list "signs that a workplace is psychologically unsafe." Next, have them list "signs of a psychologically safe workplace." Then work with the team to identify actions you and the team can take to promote a psychologically safe work environment. Be sure to ask the team if there are things you have done to make them feel unsafe and if there are things you could do to make things safer.
- Think about a "do-over moment" you wish you could have as a leader. How were your emotions at play in the situation? What regrets do you have about how you handled or mis-handled things? If you were to have a "do-over," what would you do differently?
- Learn more about McKinsey's "obligation to dissent." mckinsey.com/about-us/overview/our-purpose-mission-and-values.
- Read *The Fearless Organization: Creating Psychological Safety in the Workplace for Learning, Innovation, and Growth*, by Amy C. Edmondson (Wiley Publishing, 2018).

BONUS TIP

Just like people in any healthy relationship, your team will want to know whether you'll be there for them when the chips are down. There will come a time when a more senior leader from outside your team questions the quality of its work, its speed, or its rigid fidelity to company processes and standards. At some point, your team's work is bound to be under siege by a more senior leader who isn't your boss. As a new leader, you may be tempted to quickly "side" with that leader out of deference to his or her rank.

Instead, first ask clarifying questions to better understand the merits of the leader's point of view. Often, you'll discover that your team is, in fact, doing everything correctly, but its accurate work is somehow interfering with the work the outside leader is responsible for. If so, let the leader know, soberly and courageously, all additional context or facts they may not be aware of. If they aren't satisfied with your answer, tell them you're happy to arrange a meeting so you, your boss, and the leader can explore options for creating efficiencies between your team and the team they lead.

Here's the two-word bonus tip for creating safety when your team is under misguided attack from leaders outside the team:

PROVIDE AIRCOVER

CHAPTER 9

NURTURE TALENT

Develop People So They Can Add More Value

I once led a leadership workshop for a group of seasoned leaders in Chicago. Near the end of the session, one of the leaders said, "Bill, I get what you're saying, and the content has been a great reminder of what I should be doing to be a better leader. So much of what you covered today has to do with taking an interest in developing the people I'm responsible for leading. I want to be a better leader, Bill, I really do. I just don't have the time." Other heads were nodding in agreement, so I asked him to elaborate.

He continued, "Years ago, I could set aside one-on-one time each week for each of my direct reports. I had the luxury of being able to draw out their questions so I could give thoughtful answers. I could explain the "why" behind some of the organization's initiatives and goals. I could go out to lunch with the team and enjoy getting to know everyone personally. It was fun watching people grow while growing myself in the process. Now, though, everything is compressed. The leaders above me are under more pressure for more profits; they constantly fire off urgent requests to me and my team adding unrealistic deadlines. Every day I'm being asked to do more but being given less with which to do it. Lunch? Forget it. The best I can do is eat a Subway sandwich while trying to knock out more work. Who can develop people when you're punching out work, tethered to your computer like it was a respirator?"

Today's workplace is littered with jaded leaders who have gotten so subsumed by work that they've lost sight of one of the greatest responsibilities and joys that a leader has: nurturing talent. A leader is successful to the extent that they help those they are leading to be successful.

Yes, you are busy. Yes, you have big responsibilities and demanding bosses and clients. Yes, your home life often competes with your work life. Tough noogies. You don't get a pass from the central leadership requirement for developing your people. In earlier chapters, you learned techniques for delegating, managing time, and building trust. Those techniques will help you help them. People need your time, attention, and guidance so they can do their best. Investing your time and drawing out their capabilities ensures that they can add more value to the organization and have fulfilling careers. After working with you, each of your direct reports should be somehow enhanced, better off for having been positively impacted by your leadership. It's kinda the whole point of leadership, right?

CREATE OPPORTUNITY

One of the best ways to nurture talent is to give people work opportunities that use every bit of their current skills while activating latent skills you saw could be developed. It needs to be an opportunity that they view as an opportunity. Meaning, an assignment that is aligned with their passion, interest, and natural strengths, which you learned about as you got to know them better (remember Ken Blanchard's fifteen minutes?). The reason for this is they'll be more into it, fully engaged with the opportunity because they view it as benefitting them and their career. They'll have more ownership, investment, and energy to take advantage of the opportunity.

Opportunity jazzes people. Think about how this has worked in your own career. There likely was some leader who took the time to get to know your interests, and based on that, gave you an opportunity to prove yourself to yourself. They recognized your latent talents and gave you a shot at developing them. They believed in you long enough for you to start believing in yourself. It's likely that you wouldn't even be where you are today in your career had it not been for that leader's influence on you. Well, guess what? Now it is your leadership duty to be fully interested in the development of your direct reports by giving them growth opportunities that nurture their abilities. This is the great tradition of leadership. The best way to honor the leaders who have had a positive impact on you is for you to have a positive impact on those you're now leading.

During my company's leadership workshops, we have people write down in a single word the sentiment they hold for those "opportunity leaders" who made all the difference in their lives. Then we have them shout out the words. "Belief!" "Gift!" "Mentor!" and "Gratitude!" they'll say. Then we ask the class to imagine that it's three years from now and it's a new class of leaders attending the workshop: their current direct reports. Would their direct reports use similar words to describe their feelings about them?

How about you? What word would you use to describe the sentiment you hold for the leader who has made all the difference in your life or career? Do you think the people you're leading today would use a similar word to describe their feelings about you?

ORGANIC OPPORTUNITIES

You might be thinking, "Well, I'd give people opportunities if there were any to give. I can't just promote people when there are no spots to promote them into." Broaden your thinking. There are plenty of ways to grow people's skills with normal, everyday work opportunities. Here are a few:

Gulp Goals: Goals motivate people when they are both exciting and scary. Work with each of your direct reports to establish a few aggressive, but achievable, goals that cause them to go, "Gulp!" More on Gulp Goals in chapter 13.

Decision Input: When consequential decisions need to be made, invite direct reports into the evaluation process. By letting their thinking influence your thinking, you show them how much you value their minds.

Extracurricular Activities: You'll often come across one-off assignments that are important, temporary, and perfect for the involvement and development of one or two of your team members. Examples might include organizing the company's summer outing or annual fundraiser. All the better if the assignment introduces them to other leaders in the organization, so they can broaden their network while bringing attention to their talents.

Meeting Facilitation: If your team has a standing weekly meeting, consider rotating the facilitator role so each person gets to experience the leader role. Work with that person to set the agenda and define the desired meeting outcomes. Then let them sit in the leader seat while you join the rest of the team.

Proxy Yourself: When you go on vacation (and please do!), assign a different one of your direct reports to assume your role. Set clear boundaries as to what they can and can't do, and make it clear to the rest of the team what those boundaries are. Also make it clear to the team that you expect them to support the leader, and for the leader to support the team. This is an entry-level way of preparing your eventual successor.

The point is for you to constantly strive for ways to grow and develop each of your direct reports, using organically occurring opportunities that are natural to the work environment. It's not about giving people promotions; it's about advancing their skills and deepening their experience.

DELEGATE WILLFULLY

In chapter 4 you learned how delegating is one of the essentials for managing your time more effectively. That's true. But delegation serves a more important function: it's a powerful way to develop your people.

A lot of leadership careers plateau due to a lack of delegation skills. The leader gets mired in tasks they've outgrown but is unwilling to release. Sometimes they argue that there is no one else capable of doing the task or doing it up to the necessary standards. More often the real reasons are that they a) actually enjoy performing the task, or b) are afraid of losing the visibility or importance that comes with the task.

Those who do learn how to delegate often do so because of reluctant surrendering. They become so swamped that they bottleneck work progress until they cry "uncle" and start tagging off tasks to their direct reports' capable hands. The most common refrain I hear from my coaching clients who have struggled with delegation is, "I wish I had done it sooner. Things didn't fall apart as I was so sure would happen. I guess I wasn't holding the world together the way I assumed I was!"

Delegation is not going to hurt you. It's going to help you. And it's going to help you help the people you're leading. By delegating substantive, meaningful, and important tasks, you develop more of their skills. When it works right, there's a certain positive mutual incrementalism at work, where the delegated assignment frees you up to take on higher-order tasks while simultaneously building their skills so they can become capable of performing even bigger tasks, which frees you up even more, and so on. By nurturing and developing their talents through delegation, both you and they come to add more value to the organization.

Readiness is the key to delegation: your readiness to let go and their readiness to grab hold. Start by listing all the tasks for which you're responsible. Consider using the time management process you were introduced to in chapter 4 to identify tasks taking an inordinate amount of your attention. Next, identify tasks you've outgrown, or that are so easy for you that you'll regress if you don't delegate them—be honest. Also identify the tasks that you absolutely need to retain, either because you're still mastering them or because they are a foundational part of your role (such as reviewing the work of your direct reports). You may be surprised to discover through this process that there are some tasks you may be able to eliminate altogether. Think of this as your stop-doing list.

Once you have the list of items to delegate, identify those to whom you can delegate, considering such things as who on the team has a workload that could withstand the new assignment, whose skills would benefit from the task, and how much support and training the person will need so they can successfully perform the task.

Readiness is the key to delegation: your readiness to let go, and their readiness to grab hold.

Next, meet with the person to whom you're delegating, and clarify the importance of the task and how doing it is the next logical progression in their career growth. Let them know the results they will need to achieve, and by when those results are expected. Discuss their initial ideas about doing the work, offering your guidance where needed. Finally, agree upon a "check-in" date so you can see how things are going, and give additional support as needed. Be clear that they can reach out to you whenever they have a question or if progress stalls.

Finally, once they've taken hold of the task, you may feel a strong pull toward "helping" them by offering additional input and direction. Once or twice is okay; three times is meddling.

RECOGNIZE PROGRESS

Always remember that learning something new (i.e., "development") is generally uncomfortable. Therefore, creating safety, the focus of the prior chapter, happens as a precursor to development—safe work environments increase people's willingness to try new things. You may, for example, delegate something that you could now do in your sleep. But for the person you're assigning it to, they may be afraid of messing up or letting you down. That's normal and necessary. People don't grow in a zone of comfort. They grow, progress, and evolve in a zone of discomfort. Part of your responsibility as a leader is to support people as you ask them to take on harder tasks. Sometimes your job will be to make people uncomfortable, in a good way.

Often, learning is a mistake-prone, two-steps-forward, one-step-back process, full of self-doubt and setbacks. They're going to scrape their knees a little, and as they do, you need to have their backs. Your encouragement of their development becomes extra important when learning gets rocky, as it inevitably does.

When people extend themselves, try new and uncomfortable things, and take appropriate risks, be sure to recognize it. Take them aside and say, "I'm really proud of you. That took a lot of courage and effort, and I'm sure it wasn't comfortable. Doing things like that will help you go a long way." Then say, "thank you," and mean it. Because when they extend themselves and grow and develop, they add more value, directly benefitting you and the organization.

TRY COURAGE

It's time to learn about the third behavioral expression of courage. This is about intentionally moving outside of one's comfort zone to attempt something new. It's called TRY Courage because it involves trying new things, and it is mostly about having initiative and taking action in the face of discomfort.

TRY Courage is what you're talking about when you want people to "step up to the plate." You see it during first attempts when people do things for the first time at work. Often, your direct reports have never done the tasks you're delegating to them. It makes sense that the assignment will be uncomfortable for them. There's a risk, after all, that they could fail. Thus, TRY Courage is what it will take for the person to attempt the task while assuming the risk of failure. Their discomfort will subside as they gain proficiency with the new task.

Here are a few quick tips for promoting TRY Courage:

Model Courage: Make sure you occasionally attempt new tasks or activities in front of your team. Be the first one up and off the high dive ladder. Jump first!

Recall History: Remind the person of other uncomfortable work tasks or activities they completed successfully.

Envision Success: Spend time with them envisioning and clarifying a successful outcome. Focus on the things they'll need to get right versus what could go wrong.

Praise Mistakes: People are bound to make a few goofs as they're learning new tasks or attempting new things. Mistakes are elemental to the learning process, so praise mistakes when people make them. It's only when mistakes become habitual or egregious that your reaction should shift.

Normalize Discomfort: Let people know that feeling uncomfortable is a normal and natural part of the learning process. Help them become comfortable with discomfort.

The last chapter was all about creating safety. The reason it preceded this chapter is that people generally feel afraid when extending themselves, attempting new things, and taking career risks—all of which you need them to do in pursuit of strong results. Creating safety increases their willingness to move into their discomfort zone, where the learning happens, and where TRY Courage will be on display!

REGULARIZE FEEDBACK

It's shocking how many organizations still don't have a process for providing regular performance feedback. Even those who do, often pencil-whip the process, viewing it as a necessary inconvenience. The lack of feedback is rife at all levels. I once coached the director of a nonprofit who hadn't gotten performance feedback from her board in five years. That's criminal. No employee should be left to grope in the dark, unsure about the contribution or progress they're making.

Sometimes people only get feedback when they do something wrong and hear the groans of their bosses. Leadership by negative exception is a recipe for high turnover. Who only wants to hear about what they're bad at all the time?

Some performance review systems are designed as a once-a-year process so all the feedback gets backed up like a septic tank ready to explode all over the employee. People often leave review meetings demoralized and frustrated that they weren't made aware of performance deficiencies far earlier in the year so they could have taken corrective action. For all the "no surprises" haranguing that bosses do, they seem to ditch the advice when it comes to doing performance reviews.

You can do better. You can give feedback frequently and routinely as part of the development process. It doesn't have to be a big deal. It's as simple as regularly reinforcing the good stuff you see and coaching the not-so-good-stuff. Good or not good, it helps to first ask the person how they thought they did before offering your input. Simply say, "How do you think it went?" They're smart. Just like you, they mostly know when they did well and when they didn't. Let them do some of the processing. Then you chime in afterward, always aiming to be helpful and inspire improvement.

CHUG BEER

Even excellent performers occasionally make mistakes, say something inappropriate, or violate company standards. When they do, you must confront it. It will be one of the most challenging aspects of your job because it's largely an uncomfortable and one-way conversation. It helps to have a specific structure to guide the feedback. One useful and memorable approach was first suggested by Dan McCarthy, a seasoned leadership expert whose website, GreatLeadershipByDan.com, offers sound and time-tested advice. When corrective feedback is needed, Dan suggests having a **BEER** with your direct report. Now, before you turn me in to HR, let me clarify that he's talking about a process, not a refreshing liquid that inspires awkward dancing.

Behavior: Explain what the person is doing or not doing and why it's not acceptable.

Effect: Talk about the negative effects the behavior is having on people or performance. Include the worse effects that will likely occur if corrective action isn't taken.

Expectation: Remind the person about the standards you expect or clarify the action you expect them to take immediately to confront the issue.

Result: Using a positive tone, paint a picture of how things will be better once they take corrective action.

BEER is a memorable framework to guide you during the rare times when you'll have to give tough corrective feedback, best not used with alcohol!

DEVELOPMENT WORKS

One of the advantages of a thirty-year career is accumulating enough evidence to support your convictions. Some people doubt that training can develop leadership skills. They think that people are either born with what it takes to be a leader, or they aren't. Early on, I harbored my own doubts about the impact such training could truly have.

Leadership did seem to come more naturally to some people than others.

Now, though, benefitting from thirty years of evidence, I know leadership development works. In fact, one of my most satisfying moments was watching a group of vice presidents deliver their division's business plan during a strategic offsite planning meeting. I had worked with many of those VPs from before they assumed their first leadership roles. I knew them before they were versed in the company jargon, back when they would get nervous when answering a simple question in a workshop. And now here they were, business-minded professionals presenting their plans, full of knowledge and confidence. I found myself welling up with pride as I reflected on how far each had come.

Bear in mind that it wasn't just me who had contributed to the development of those leaders. The leaders who had led them played a huge role in their advancement. There had been scores of one-on-one developmental meetings, stretch assignments, sidebar feedback conversations, and performance reviews. Whatever natural leadership acumen each person may have started with was far outweighed by the nurturing attention each leader had been given along the

Leading since **2008**

Tom Tucker

Vice President, Aldridge Electric Incorporated

You need to really care about and believe in what you are doing. There will be difficult days, problems that feel impossible and strained relationships with your team. Staying true to caring about the work and the project teams has always kept me on the path to push through, keep my cool, and get to the finish line.

way. Not a single person in that room, from the VPs to their bosses, had gotten there alone. Each had benefitted from the baton-passing tradition that leadership is, as more experienced leaders support, develop, and coach new leaders along their journey. Leaders creating leaders is what leadership is all about.

THINK NOW/*ACT NOW*

Think Now

Who is a leader who invested time in you? What has the payoff been for that investment?

What are some key work opportunities you've been given over the years and how did they help you grow and develop?

What has been your experience with delegating thus far? How might it benefit you to delegate more? How could you use delegation to develop the people you're leading?

Think about a leader you worked with who did an excellent job of providing feedback, whether in the form of positive recognition or corrective feedback. What did they do or say that built your reception to the feedback? What could you emulate and carry forward into your feedback conversations with your direct reports?

Act Now

- List some "organic opportunities" you could involve your direct reports in today.
- Go through the exercise described in this chapter of identifying what and to whom you should delegate. Also create a stop-doing list—activities or tasks you can eliminate.
- Meet with each person to whom you're delegating a new task to ensure a smooth transition. Be sure to monitor progress on the task until it's confidently performed.

- Make time to privately recognize people who are stretching and challenging themselves by learning new and uncomfortable things!

BONUS TIP

When you move into a new leadership role, you start to develop a broader and more influential network. While that network will be good for your career, you can also tap into it for the good of your team's careers. When your team is getting ready to launch a substantial new work effort or when it reaches a significant milestone, ask your boss to visit with your team to acknowledge their good work. Doing so creates a direct line of sight between the team's work and your boss's eyes, and lets the team know that others besides you see them as important.

Your two-word bonus tip is:

GIVE ACCESS

CHAPTER 10

PROMOTE INCLUSION

Create a Just, Fair, and Equitable Workplace

Let's do a little exercise. For five minutes, write down the many ways you would describe yourself—for example, your features, profession, religion, marital or relationship status, circle of friends, favorite recreational activities, political affiliation, and personality characteristics. Review your description.

Imagine it's a year from now and I'm having you do the same exact exercise. What are the chances that you'd give me the same exact words? I'm guessing very slim. You may go through a breakup or divorce; you may meet new friends, or pick up a new hobby. Over the course of a single year, some parts of your identity fluctuate while other parts remain seemingly fixed. Even those that seem fixed are subject to change. Though it's rare, you may change religions or political parties, for example. You may take a DNA test and find that your heritage includes strands from ethnicities your relatives never told you about. Even your cells are constantly regenerating, and every seven years or so your entire body is made up of cells that weren't there seven years before. You are not static. You are complex, and ever-changing, singularly diverse. Yes, you are an individual, but you are made up of many ingredients.

Imagine too, that each one of the people you are leading did the same activity. How likely is it that they would have the same exact words as you? For that matter, how likely is it that they'd have the same exact words as any other team member? Not likely at all. Because they too are singularly diverse, each an individual and each full of difference and dimension.

Not only are all of you personally and collectively diverse but you also change daily. Some days you're upbeat, energetic, and ready to go. Others you're blasé, lethargic, and ready to go to sleep. We change frequently in other ways too, from our waist sizes to our hair length and color to the styles we wear.

To deny diversity is to deny reality.

BLIND BIASES

While we are all blessedly different, we generally want similar things: to be treated fairly and respectfully, to be included, heard, and valued, to be emotionally supported and encouraged, and to be recognized and thanked for our contributions. All of us want to be treated like our lives matter as much as everyone else's, and that we are not invisible. We don't feel like we should have to earn these things. They are the minimum basic standards we expect as human beings—our human rights. And we especially expect these rights to be acknowledged, upheld, and protected by the people who lead us. You.

Leadership comes with power and privilege. When you are in a leadership role you can impact your direct reports' progression, compensation, and, for better or for worse, career trajectory. Being able to impact a person's promotability gives you a lot of power. Regardless of how "good" you believe yourself to be as a human being, if you are blind to your own biases, you'll also be blind to all the ways those biases may favor some people while negatively impacting others.

You do have biases. Everyone does. Bias, in simple terms, is the tendency to favor one thing over another. Some biases are completely harmless. I remember the first Thanksgiving dinner I had with my wife's family. As I made my way through the kitchen, I glanced over at the casserole dish with the sweet potatoes and made the mistake of saying, "When are you toasting the marshmallow topping and adding the candied pecans?" My comment was met with scornful looks and groans. I never would have guessed that the woman I love grew up in a family that didn't sweeten their sweet potatoes! "Jeez," I thought to myself, "the poor family has been deprived of a real sweet potato casserole, the way it's supposed to be." I still pity their deprivation.

Other biases are more problematic because they cause us to either favor certain people or they interfere with our ability to give others fair treatment. I'm convinced that the main reason I got my first job in organizational development was that the woman interviewing me was, like me, a graduate of West Virginia University. While I did my best to embellish my then very thin resume, the fact that the interviewer and I were fellow WVU Mountaineers created an instant kinship. I got the job, which, thankfully, set my career on its way so I could get the experience I lacked. I don't begrudge my fellow Mountaineer for giving me the opportunity. Why would I? I am just realistic about the invisible factors that tipped employment in my favor.

While I've been the beneficiary of the favoritism of others, my own biases have interfered with how I've treated others. As a fast-talking suburban New Yorker, when I first moved to the South, I judged the intelligence of others by the speed at which they talked. The more I had to wait for a southerner to finish a sentence, the more dimwitted I was sure the other person was... and treated them as such. That is, until I started working for a boss who was born and raised in Mississippi. He broke every stereotype I held about the South, and, to this day, remains not only a mentor to me, but the smartest and most level-headed, good-natured, and principled leader I've ever met.

To be fair, I'm sure my southern friends stereotyped my New York aggressiveness too. I'm sure that after many interactions, some of my southern friends would whisper, "Bless his little Yankee heart."

ET TU?

More dangerous biases are those that we don't know we have—or convince ourselves that we don't. Most of us like to believe we are "neutral," unaffected by bias. Even if we are aware of our biases, we generally don't want to admit to them. Who wants to stand up and say, "You know those [insert a gender, race, religion, ethnicity, or political affiliation]? I'm prejudiced against them!"

To illustrate the potential for bias, imagine for a moment that you're leading a small project team of graphic designers for a software company. Your team has just taken on a big new project and you and your boss agree it's time to recruit a new team member. You've interviewed several candidates and no one has impressed you enough to want to hire them. You're scheduled to meet with another candidate this afternoon.

You're not quite sure how to react when you meet the candidate, Melanie, at the front of the building. She extends her left hand to introduce herself, which is unusual. Her right arm is bent, with her forearm held upright and her fist clenched. Her head is unsteady, as if it were balanced on a swivel, though her eyes remain fixed. Her gait is more of a teeter, with her right foot turned inward, making it seem like she is going to tip over sideways at any moment.

The interview takes longer than it did with the other candidates. Melanie's face becomes distorted as she speaks, and each of her words requires more of your attention to process than you're used to. She also is wearing some sort of hearing aid, but it looks different from other hearing aids you've seen before. The device is connected to a wire that is attached to a round magnet on the side of her head, about the size of a quarter. Clearly, Melanie has some physical challenges, but none that would interfere, apparently, with her work. She shows you examples of her graphics work, which is excellent. She is also friendly and professional and her answers, though they take some time to formulate, are smart. You've asked her if she would need any accommodations to work for you, and other than patience with her pace, she said "no."

I ask you honestly, would you hire Melanie? Would you want to talk to your boss first? Would you want to confer with HR? Your company's legal team? Why the hesitancy? She already told you she wouldn't need any accommodations. Why would hiring Melanie seem riskier than hiring any other person?

What if she did ask for accommodations? What if, for example, she asked for a particular type of phone, chair, or computer. So what? Would it really be that hard to work with your company to make those things available? Most sizable organizations can easily provide such things. In fact, by law, they are required to.

It's easy to reject things you have no direct experience with, including people. The opposite is also true. We accept what we know. Familiarity reduces ignorance. You can witness this in people's personal lives. The racism of parents often shrinks when, for example, their son or daughter marries a person of another race. The transformation isn't overnight, and not without arguments, defensiveness, and soul-searching. But eventually, the parents become caring in-laws to the spouse and loving grandparents to biracial grandkids. Likewise, a person may go out of their way to avoid people with autism, intellectual disabilities, cerebral palsy, or hearing impairments...until they learn their child is affected by one of them. As a parent, they often become a great protector of the rights of the people whose differences they once avoided. As a leader, you should purposely seek out people whose life experiences are different from your own, if for no other reason than to reduce your own bias and ignorance.

I would hope that you'd hire Melanie, because you'd be hiring someone very much like my own daughter, Tobina. Bina, as we know her, has cerebral palsy (CP) and is profoundly deaf. CP is a movement disorder, and the right side of Bina's body is stiff—similar to people who have had a stroke. She wears a cochlear implant, a high-tech hearing aid that enables her to hear and talk. And work. She was the first of my three children to become gainfully employed, which she is fond of reminding her two brothers, neither of whom have disabilities. Though she does not require any special allowances at work, I thank God that she is protected by federal laws through the Americans with Disabilities Act (ADA) in case she ever does. You'd be thankful too if you had a child with a disability. I'm betting you'd be your child's fiercest defender.

INCLUSION'S OPPOSITE

One of my favorite people in the world is Gloria Cotton, a diversity and inclusion expert based in Chicago. I met Gloria some years back when one of my clients brought her in to work with a group of leaders. The audience was almost entirely made up of white, middle-aged males. More than a few had their arms folded, with skeptical faces that said, "Lady, don't even try to change me." But slowly, as Gloria engaged the group, the folded arms came down, and the grumpy faces gave way to smiles. More importantly, people began engaging around a topic they normally tiptoe around.

I've come to love Gloria for her personhood. She has a way of disarming people and inviting them to talk about things they often avoid. She doesn't bristle or shame people when they ask ignorant but innocent questions. Instead, she moves into the question, exploring it with the person from various vantage points, until the person can conclude for themselves the answers that are morally right. She's fun too! Often telling a person that their question is "delicious," or when someone says something particularly vulnerable and honest, she'll say, "Baby, there's a hug in your future...if you want one."

As Gloria points out, most people don't consciously intend to exclude others. Most people think of themselves as good people. Nobody goes home at night and says, "I can't wait to go to work tomorrow so I can offend everyone!" Despite that, she notes, on surveys and in exit interviews, many people report feeling left out, unheard, and unsupported at work. There is sometimes a sizable disconnect between the good intentions of leaders and the actual experiences of the people who work for them. Gloria advises leaders to remember these four points about inclusion:

1. Inclusion is not a spectator sport. You must do the work to be in the game.
2. Intent and impact are two different things. What works for me may not work for others.
3. We are all inclusive of who we are inclusive of. The question is, why aren't many people inclusive of all people?
4. We may strive to treat everyone equally. But people need to be treated equitably to feel they are seen and valued as individuals.

One of the ways Gloria invites people to consider how they might be unintentionally excluding others is to share simple stories of times when she has done so. One story involves a harmless pair of scissors, with Gloria role-playing herself and a coworker named Jim. The dialogue goes something like this:

Jim: Good afternoon, Gloria. I need your help with something. Can you sign off on this invoice for me?

Gloria: Hi, Jim. What's the invoice for?

Jim: I need to order a pair of left-handed scissors for myself.

Gloria: *(to herself) STOP THE PRESSES! What is he talking about? There's no such thing as left-handed scissors. There's just scissors! Is he scamming me?*

Gloria: Did you lose or break the scissors that came with your office set up?

Jim: No.

Gloria: Well, then, what's the problem?

Jim: Do you have your scissors?

Gloria: Yes. I have MY scissors.

Jim: Indulge me for a minute. Take out a sheet of paper and cut it in half with your scissors.

Gloria: Really, man? OK. *(After Gloria cut the paper, Jim continued.)*

Jim: Now, place the scissors in your left hand and cut those two pieces of paper in half.

Gloria: *(to herself) How much longer is THIS ridiculousness going to last? Bless his heart!*

Then something strange happened. Gloria didn't even know how to hold the scissors. Not only did it feel awkward but she also didn't even know how to approach the task. Instantly her colleague's request made sense.

Gloria: Is this what it feels like when you're using this right-handed scissors?

Jim: Yes.
Gloria: What else do you need that's made for left-handed people?!

It's a simple story with a powerful impact. Gloria, like most people, is right-handed. She assumed that everyone used scissors the same way. It didn't even occur to her that the design of most scissors was exclusively fitted for right-handed people. That was the "standard." That was "normal." Her brief exchange with Jim taught her a lifelong lesson that she now carries to others: What's normal for one person may be a hindrance for another.

INSTITUTIONAL BIAS

It will take you about twenty seconds of internet research to find studies on the negative impact of bias in the workplace. It will be twenty seconds well spent, particularly if you take additional time to thoroughly read the studies. One famous study from 2016, involved resume screening processes at companies throughout the United States. Researchers created resumes for entry-level jobs and posted them on job websites in sixteen metropolitan areas. The resumes included email addresses and phone numbers, which had been set up by the researchers. The content of the resumes was identical, except some contained racial cues indicating that an applicant was Black or Asian. Callbacks for resumes that included ethnic information were dramatically lower than those that didn't, despite the actual credentials being identical.

The study also demonstrated that African American and Asian job applicants who mask their resumes by deleting clues to their race—referred to as "whitening"—fare better at getting job interviews than those who don't.* Many applicants change their name, for example, replacing "Lei" with

*Sonia K. Kang et al., "Whitened Resumes: Race and Self-Presentation in the Labor Market," *Administrative Science Quarterly*, 61, no. 3 (March 2016).

Leading since 1990

Gloria Cotton

Senior Partner, inQUEST Consulting

Being a "good person" is not enough. Our behaviors and actions make the real difference. Leaders need to be intentional in their treatment of people. Every human being wants to, deserves to, and is entitled to be welcomed, valued, respected, heard, understood, and supported. Doing that is what it means to be pro-inclusive.

"Luke" to Americanize it. Others will include interests that would normally be associated with white cultures, such as tennis, snowboarding, and whitewater kayaking. The research suggests minorities whiten their resumes for good reason: it works. Companies are twice as likely to call back applicants who submit whitened resumes as those who reveal their race. This discriminatory practice was just as strong for companies that actively encouraged applications from underrepresented minority groups as for those who didn't. This is particularly harmful because many minority applicants are more transparent about their racial identity when applying to jobs at companies that say they welcome and promote diversity but in practice still discriminate.

The researchers conclude that it is unlikely that pro-diversity companies that actively recruit minority candidates are intentionally putting up barriers that simultaneously exclude them. More likely, the implicit biases of the individuals who quickly screen the resumes are at play.

Similar studies, by the way, have been done to assess workplace gender discrimination. When identical application materials are submitted, the applicants with male names are consistently rated as more hirable and competent than those with female names. They also earmark male applicants for higher-paying jobs. This was true whether the evaluator assessing the application was male or female.

DIVERSITY BENEFITS

Promoting diversity is the right thing to do. But diversity also has brass-tack business benefits.

More Candidates: One frequent complaint from new leaders is that there are never enough people to get all the work done. When the economy is good and the labor market becomes even more competitive, it becomes especially difficult to hire additional talent. Among the many reasons it's important to illuminate your own hidden biases is to avoid excluding job candidates who could help you and your organization. The bigger the talent pool you're drawing from, the more likely it is that you'll hire someone who can help you advance your goals. Call it enlightened self-interest.

Better Ideas: Innovation and group performance go up in direct proportion to how diverse a team is. It makes sense. If everyone has similar personality dispositions, we're likely to view problems similarly and land on similar ideas for solving them. Many design and ideation companies, for example, purposely assign people with dramatically different personality types and social backgrounds to the same team to dilate the flow of creative ideas. Constituting purposefully diverse teams is also done to prevent the dangers of "groupthink" that often typify homogenous groups. Teams that include different viewpoints and thinking styles are shown to solve problems faster and better (producing more patents, for example).

Enhanced Reputation: Think about it. Which company would you be most drawn to? One with a reputation for hiring people with diverse backgrounds and experiences, or one with as much sameness as possible? Who wants to work in Clone City? How boring would that be?! It turns out that organizations with inclusive business cultures and practices are shown to have stronger marketplace reputations. Likewise, employees who work at such companies have higher levels of trust and satisfaction, and believe their employers are more ethical.

There is ample evidence that the more diverse the organization and its practices, the better it does financially. That said, company owners who question the value of DEI never seem to be fully satisfied with whatever business rationale is put in front of them. The only "proof" that seems to get their attention is one of their diversity-embracing competitors beating them in the marketplace.

BE PRO-INCLUSION

It's not enough for you to be against racism. You've got to be pro-inclusion. Meaning, you must use your leadership power and privilege to intentionally create opportunities for others, while being especially sensitive to invisible biases that can skew your preferences and judgment. All leaders, new ones in particular, are susceptible to hiring people who look like, talk like, and think as they do. Wise leaders go out of their way to learn about the experiences of those who are least like them, so they can learn how to ally with them and advocate for them.

Despite living in the twenty-first century, sadly, there are still too many people who believe in the inferiority or inborn wrongness of others. There are still people who won't hire people of a certain skin color, accent, sexual orientation, faith, or disability. I'm hoping that's not you. If it is, I urge you to do everything in your power to change. You'll do a tremendous amount of damage in the world if you believe that your race, religion, or ethnic heritage is superior to that of others. Racism is anti-leadership.

As you're reading this, I have no idea what your gender, color, race, religion, or ethnic makeup is. You may very well already fit into a uniquely diverse profile or underrepresented minority group. Or not. Regardless, the responsibility remains the same: to ensure that you do as much as you can to reduce your biases and to treat everyone equitably and respectfully. The goal should not be to reduce your potential for doing wrong by people with your bias. It should be to increase your likelihood of doing right by everyone. Promote inclusion.

Racism is anti-leadership.

THINK NOW/*ACT NOW*

Think Now

Did you grow up with brothers and sisters? If so, was there ever a time when you felt that one or both of your parents favored one of your siblings? How did you react to that?

Have you witnessed blatant favoritism at work? As you watched it, how did it make you feel?

When have you received favoritism? Why were you favored? What outcomes emerged because of having been favored?

Have you ever favored someone at work? Why did you favor that person? What did they gain from that favoritism? What were the reactions of those who witnessed or were aware of the favoritism?

What beliefs do you hold about racism and prejudice? How might those beliefs impact your leadership and your influence on those you're leading?

Which of your direct reports is least like you? What is your perception about those differences? What is your perception of the person? How might your perceptions of the differences be impacting your perception of the person?

Act Now

- Does your organization have a person or function related to DEI? Likewise, are there explicit policies and practices in place promoting DEI? Familiarize yourself with all the ways the company is promoting DEI and commit yourself to further those efforts.
- Learn more about DEI here: dei.extension.org/.
- Project Implicit is a nonprofit organization founded by researchers and a team of scientists who research new ways of understanding attitudes, stereotypes, and hidden biases that influence perception, judgment, and action. You can take their free test here: implicit.harvard.edu/implicit/takeatest.html

- Review a ton of research on the benefits of DEI here: catalyst.org/research/why-diversity-and-inclusion-matter/#easy-footnote-bottom-7-6361
- There are many books on topics related to DEI. Get recommendations from your organization's DEI department, if it has one, or from a friend or leader who you know is committed to DEI ideals and practices.

BONUS TIP

There are lots of engaging and non-threatening ways to have a conversation with your team about diversity. One popular activity is titled I am, but I am not. It's a personal way of dispelling stereotypes and myths. Here's how it works:

On a piece of paper, draw a line down the middle, and title one side, I am. Title the other side, I am not. In the middle, put the word "but." Write 5 "I am, but I am not" statements. The "I am not" statement should be a commonly held stereotype. Before reviewing everyone's examples, emphasize the importance of listening and respect. First, share your own example to set the tone. Here's one of mine: "I am Irish, but I am not a drinker."

Have each person share their 5 examples. Other teammates should remain silent until the person sharing finishes. Process a little after each round by asking questions such as: Who else has experienced that stereotype? When did you first learn about that stereotype? How has it been reinforced during your life?

The point is to learn from one another. It's not uncommon for people to laugh, nod their heads in agreement, express surprise, or cry. The point is to create an appreciation for each person's heritage and background while valuing their uniqueness. People generally come away more appreciative of each other's differences, and more bonded—and sometimes relieved—by knowing that everyone has experienced hurtful stereotypes

Your next two-word bonus tip is:

SHARE DIFFERENCES

Leadership Oath 2
A Promise to Do Right by Others

I promise to be a good leader of others. I promise to always remember that leading others is a privilege and that I best honor that privilege by treating others with the respect and dignity they deserve as fellow human beings.

I am keenly aware that my own success as a leader is based on how well I lead them, while nurturing their unique gifts and talents, and giving them opportunities to continue to grow and advance.

I will faithfully stay vigilant against the dangers that my own biases can present and commit myself to facing them and rooting them out so that I can do right by others—my most solemn duty.

I commit myself to create an inviting environment where people can express themselves fully and where everyone is treated equitably, inclusively, and respectfully.

Being a good leader means being a good leader for others, and that's what I aim to be.

Signed: ______________________________

Date: ______________________________

PART III

LEADING WORK

You were put into a leadership role for a reason: to get things done. It's self-evident that leaders lead people. But they also lead work and all the strategies, processes, and practices that affect how well and fast that work gets done. Work will be a lot more enjoyable when you're not afraid of it. Business and the people who make business happen are often intimidating, driven by impatience and high expectations. They expect you to get results, and if you don't, they'll replace you with the next person in line who promises to. Learning the mechanics of getting work done, including sound management practices, will simultaneously remove your fear and build your business confidence. Before you know it, you'll even be able to lead the leaders who are responsible for leading you. Things will really take off for your leadership when you start to love business and all its challenges and complexities. This section aims to help you do just that.

CHAPTER 11

LOVE BUSINESS

Keep Learning and You'll Enjoy the Adventure!

The business of business is business, and leadership requires knowing it, understanding it, and loving it. This is true whether you work in the public or private sector, or a non-profit or for-profit establishment.

While the word "business" generally implies commerce, if a nonprofit or government organization isn't explicitly selling goods, that doesn't mean there isn't business involved. Many nonprofits draw billions in revenue. One government agency my company has worked with gets $24 billion per year in taxpayer funding. So, by "business" I mean how all the levers operate, the interstitial relationships between functions and departments, the markets and customers being served and the benefits they draw from that service, the customer acquisition and business development process, the flow of the funding sources and what causes them to dilate or contract, how they procure equipment and supplies, the overall risk appetite and profile and how risks are mitigated (including the legal and contract management process), and how they attract, nurture, evaluate, and reward talent, among countless other things.

Don't expect to learn this stuff all at once or even in this book. But don't expect to bypass learning it either unless you aim to flatline your leadership career. Yes, the sheer volume of all there is to learn about business is daunting and, let's face it, intimidating. Until you catch up, you'll feel pretty small when the bigwigs are tossing head-scratching words around like "monetize," "incentivize," "accretion," "modalities," and "optimize." What the heck is "EBITDA" anyway? (It's an acronym for Earnings Before Interest, Taxes, Depreciation, and Amortization, used to indicate overall profitability.)

Don't worry, not all fancy-pants words are of equal value, and some can be said in a far simpler way. (Please ditch the word "utilize" and replace it with the word "use"—they mean the same thing). Over time, the words and meanings will start to make more sense. So too will all the outer- and innerworkings of the entire enterprise. Aside from the part of the business that is under your direct leadership, you don't need to be an "expert" on the entire business. You just have to gain a clear understanding of how it all works and fits together. The more you learn and know, the less intimidating it will all be, until someday, voilà, you start to genuinely love business. This is when your leadership will really begin to excel.

DIVIDENDS EARNED

What's not to love about business? After you've made the shift from fearing business to loving it, what was once the heavy grind of work starts to become a spirited adventure, each day bringing new challenges that inspire your creativity. As you become more seasoned, your judgment becomes bolder and more decisive. Fewer problems are novel, and when they are, you face them confidently, drawing on scores of prior experiences. When everything is up in the air, you trust that you'll land on your feet. You've learned, too, that today's novel problem will provide insights and wisdom for facing future dilemmas, both adding to your organization's institutional knowledge and deepening your leadership experience.

You'll begin to be included in solving grander problems and capitalizing on bigger opportunities, and as you are, you'll gain more credibility and influence, adding potency to your leadership. Accretion indeed!

Let's not forget the camaraderie that will develop between you and the other leaders as you face adventures together. You'll challenge each other, scheme, argue and align, and collaborate with each other. Sometimes you'll compete with each other, sometimes you'll compete against each other. It's all good! Each one of you will get better in the process, forging strong and enduring bonds on the road to mutual respect.

You know what else you'll come to love? Empowering your team and helping them produce, deliver, and achieve more than they ever imagined they would. Providing people with opportunities that help them develop new skills and stretch them into higher levels of performance. Watching people you've influenced grow in ability and confidence until they, too, come to love the wild, spirited, and heroic adventures that business provides. All of this will come, eventually, because of loving business. But loving it requires learning it, and that will take years...sometimes a lot of them.

Until you retire, you'll spend more time at work than at home. You might as well choose to immerse yourself in it,

Leading since 2010

Matt Malburg

Superintendent, Aldridge Electric Incorporated

I love the challenge of business operations. It brings out a competitive spirit. Always trying to be a step ahead of our competition. Using innovation and creativity to be safer, more efficient, and more cost-effective. Giving others the opportunity and freedom to be innovative and creative to find their own success, and rewarding it, so they come to love operations too.

soaking up all it has to offer. If you open yourself to it, and if you show up each day eager to learn, business can be like a hallowed university, teaching you lessons on everything imaginable, including forecasting the future; setting bold strategies; establishing or changing culture; calculating, moderating, and mitigating risk; contract management and regulatory compliance; continuous incremental improvement; transformational innovation and change; external and internal customer service; optimizing production; and human psychology and motivation. To take advantage of everything this university has to offer, your job is to be a good student who's ready to learn.

BUSINESS INFATUATION

There's a difference between business love and infatuation. Lots of people, particularly early in their career, go gaga when they hear about a hip new wunderkind leader who's raised investor funding for a spanking new startup in an emerging industry that no one yet seems to understand. There's something invigorating about joining a creative team of folks who are defining a new business while they try to figure out what the business even is.

Who doesn't love a risk-taker, right? Who wouldn't want to make a ton of money in an IPO, buy your freedom off the work treadmill, and retire early? Taking a risk on what's cool and unproven can be exciting. Most things that involve danger are. Every now and then they work out, too. A word of warning though, shiny objects—and the people who chase them—sometimes crash. A sizable percentage of business startups fail. If you're unfamiliar with the dotcom crash of 2001 it's worth a search.

It's easy to get caught up in the allure of a sexy startup when you're being promised freedom from conventional management oversight, where you can work remotely, self-expression is esteemed, and there's a possibility of a giant financial payoff. But before placing a big career bet on a startup, dig deeper. Do your due diligence and check your motives. What IS the actual business model? How will profits be made, and how long will it take to make them? How long before the enterprise is self-sustaining and not living off investor cash? What is the three-year growth plan? Is there an exit plan in place? What are the plans for after the company is sold or goes public? What happens to the current leaders after the IPO? What happens to your job? How will working in a company like this advance your career? Do you really love the business and its operations, or are you just infatuated with the company's hip image or the potential of a financial windfall?

After digging a little deeper, you may find that the grass you had hoped was greener on the other side of the hill is just dirt.

SHOW PASSION

You love things that you care deeply about. You care about things you take a genuine interest in. The more you follow your curiosity, open your mind to learn, and get involved by rolling up your sleeves, the more business will interest and fascinate you. When you sum up love, deep caring, and genuine interest, what you get is passion—that magical elixir that distinguishes great leaders from average ones and fulfilling careers from drudgery. Passion is something that can't be faked, and businesses yearn to have more rare individuals who are possessed by it. Seasoned leaders will tell you they'd take a highly passionate person with average intelligence over a highly intelligent dispassionate person any day.

Interestingly, the word "passion" comes from the Latin passio—which means "to suffer." When you're passionate about something, you're willing to toil with it, struggle with it, and be burdened by it. When you're passionate about something, you willingly sacrifice other priorities for it, giving it your time, attention, and energy. Passion is the great separator between those who are merely competent and those who gain mastery. In every field of endeavor, be it business, music, science, warcraft, politics, or sports, the people who are willing to suffer the most are the ones who gain mastery over their fields. Successful careers are built upon, and sustained, by fiery passion.

A few weeks after the pandemic of 2020 started, during the great quarantine, I had a coaching session with Lynn, a vice president I have been coaching for a long time. We hadn't spoken since the pandemic began, so naturally, the focus of the conversation was how things were going with her leadership since then. She said, "It's been crazy. Remember the three-year strategic plan our company set last year? Well, throw that out the window. None of our current forecasts are more than three weeks out now! The other execs and I are on daily calls sharing updates about emerging CDC recommendations, trying to figure our new safety protocols, identifying where to source scarce personal protective equipment (PPE), discussing exceptions and allowances from regular processes, and setting new work-from-home guidelines and giving workforce updates. It's been wild!"

As she talked, her tone got more animated and her volume a little louder. I pointed out the obvious: "You sound really into it." She laughed and reflected that "As wild and exhausting as it's been, it's been energizing. I've loved how leadership has stepped up to this moment. In the past, we've

Leading since 1993

Beth Nyland

Corporate Poet and Cutter of C.R.A.P. (Corporate Rhetoric And Pomposity), founder of Spencer Grace, and cofounder of Story Mode

I long for all leaders—whether they're newbies or old pros—to practice more curiosity. Ask questions. Be a learner. Admit what you don't know and then go after that knowledge with a hunger to understand. I find that genuinely curious leaders listen better, see more possibilities, and experience greater growth.

talked about how safety comes first, but now we're proving that it really does. I knew I cared about our people, but I love seeing how all the other leaders care about our people too. I don't know, it's strange, I think the pandemic has made us better leaders and a better leadership team."

It's passion that helps you carry the burdens of leadership and lightens it at the same time. When you believe in the value of the work you're doing, when you care about how that work gets done and the people doing it, and when you're willing to suffer through challenges and hardships so you and others can have better days, you're leading with passion. When you love business, you're a passionate leader.

PACE YOURSELF

As a new leader, you'll often feel overwhelmed, like you need to know it all now. No matter how hard you prepare, you feel, somehow, unprepared. You sit in on meetings with people who outrank you and you're afraid of getting called on. You give your direct reports tasks that you often haven't ever performed, and fear they'll ask you questions that you can't answer. You see some of your peers getting promoted and making more money, and you are partly happy for them and partly unhappy for yourself. You know you need a vacation, but how can you take one when there's so much to know? All this is happening on the good workdays and doesn't even factor into the days when stuff goes wrong and you and your team become firefighters putting out raging work emergencies. Some days feel like you're drinking from the proverbial firehose, praying that you and your team are just one project away from tranquility.

On those days when you're feeling overwhelmed or somehow inadequate, don't carry the burden alone. In the

Leading since 2011

Chris Weir

Senior Project Manager, Aldridge Electric Incorporated

As a young leader, don't be afraid to ask for help from your boss. ninety-nine percent of the time they'll be happy to get involved and provide their input. All you have to do is initiate the conversation. Asking for help is not a sign of a weak leader, it's the sign of a strong one. Nobody can do it all by themselves.

same way that one of your primary jobs as a leader is to support your direct reports, your leader's job is to support you. If you need to know something she knows, ask her. If you need more support to get things done, make your case. If you didn't understand some strange term you heard a higher-up say, just ask. Your boss is an important resource that you should draw upon frequently.

Here's a suggestion: pace yourself! You won't, can't, and shouldn't learn everything there is to know about business yet. Yes, there will be occasional emergencies that require a sprint to the finish line. But most days all you need to do is suit up, show up, and run your daily leg of the marathon. In love and business, strong foundations take time to establish and solidify. Let your love of business be a slow burn so you don't burn out. Don't rush things. Only fools do that. Elvis said so.

THINK NOW/*ACT NOW*

Think Now

What about business do you currently find intimidating?

What were some business words or phrases that you didn't initially understand but now do?

What are you starting to really enjoy, or even love, about business?

When was the last time you asked your boss for help or support? How did it go? What additional support or input would be worth asking for?

Act Now

- Make a list of all the things you don't yet know about the company you're working for but feel that you need to know. Prioritize the list, then start reaching out to the people who can assist you with beefing up your knowledge of that area, function, task, or role.
- Identify one talent or role-related responsibility that you know you're exceptional at. Next, identify two or three actions you can take to bring even greater mastery to it.
- Read *Loving Your Business: Rethink Your Relationship with Your Company and Make it Work for You*, by Debbie King (Lioncrest Publishing, 2020).

BONUS TIP

Get involved in whatever field of practice your professional discipline is dedicated to. There are associations for every occupation under the sun. Most are great avenues for networking and sharing and gaining knowledge. Sure, you'll eat a lot of rubber-textured chicken at the monthly dinners, and you'll occasionally be pestered for business by other association members, but overall, being part of an association is a great way to stay abreast of industry trends and changes so you can stay contemporary in your field.

So,

GET ASSOCIATED

CHAPTER 12

GET RESULTS

Leaders get results. You could make a good argument that results are the main reason leadership, as a concept, even exists. It is so central to leadership that it is your primary leadership responsibility, and as long as you are in a leadership role, that responsibility will drive you and those you are leading. To the extent that you get results, consistently and bountifully, your job as a leader will be secure. The opposite is also true. If you don't get results, your leadership career is toast.

The key question for your bosses when evaluating you for a leadership role is: Can you make it happen? "It" is whatever needs to be attained, achieved, or produced, and that result is the name of the game. When you can be trusted to make it happen, a lot of other leadership inadequacies will be forgiven. You might talk too much, come off as arrogant, or have a lot of turnover on your team, but if you produce results, all that will be largely overlooked. It shouldn't be that way, and I wish it weren't, but that's the way it often works.

Early on, the pressure to get results may gnaw at you, making you toss and turn at night. The pressure may spill over into arguments with your spouse or cause you to bite your nails down to nubs. It may, and probably will, cause you to take on too much yourself. None of that is constructive, and none of that will make a difference. You still have to make results happen if you want to remain in a leadership role. It is what it is, so do what you've got to do: deliver results.

DANGER AHEAD

The pressure to deliver results is as old as leadership itself. Greek mythology tells the story of Dionysius, a Sicilian king, and Damocles, his fawning courtier. Damocles had a habit of going on and on about how fortunate the king was, how magnificent he must be to have such a blessed role, and how wonderful all that power and authority must feel. Dionysius, knowing how utterly ignorant Damocles was about the actual pressures of being king—particularly the pressure to get results—generously offered to switch roles with Damocles for a day.

Damocles eagerly accepted the offer—who wouldn't want to be king for a day, right? Surrounded by every luxury, Damocles ascended to the throne. Almost as soon as he was seated, he noticed a sword hanging high above the throne, held at the sword's pommel by a single hair of a horse's tail, ready to fall and behead him at any moment. Unbeknownst to Damocles, Dionysius had arranged to have the sword suspended above the throne as a way of viscerally illustrating the invisible pressures of his job. Before assuming his temporary kingly duties, Damocles had no idea that day in, day out, Dionysius had been working under such intense threat. The king's job had seemed cushy and attractive, yet all the visible spoils of leadership were masking the tradeoff, in the form of relentless performance pressure that those spoils required. Soon Damocles buckled under the pressure, begging Dionysius to switch back to his courtier role.

For thousands of years, the Sword of Damocles has been used as a metaphor to signify the invisible pressure and threat that comes with being a leader in a position of power. Shakespeare extended the metaphor further, waxing poetic, "Uneasy lies the head that wears the crown."

Chances are, you will never be a king or queen. But if you're in a leadership role of any size or stature, because of the perilous pressure to get results, you'll often have a foreboding sense that you, too, are working perilously under an unstable, drawn and sharpened sword.

PERSIST INTENTIONALLY

One of the most rewarding aspects of leadership is when, with hard work and a strong sense of intention, a leader inspires a team of people to bring about meaningful and positive changes that make a true impact on people's lives. I was recently interviewed by a podcaster and emerging leader who has done that many times in her short career. Her impressive story made me eager to interview her for this book.

Rehnuma Karim grew up in Bangladesh in a Muslim society and always felt a need to rebel against the socially constructed expectations that were often imposed on a girl. She unknowingly began her journey towards leadership as a child when, instead of playing with other girls and dolls, she hung around with the boys, cycling and playing cricket and soccer. She rallied the neighborhood kids into organizing a mini-Olympics and launched a library for the neighborhood children in her garage. Despite occasional complaints that she was a "wild girl," her dad always encouraged her to see herself not as a girl, but first as a human being who has the power to do anything she wanted. "Follow your heart," he would tell her.

Her intention to make a positive impact became clearer with her first job experience at UNICEF Bangladesh. As a fresh college graduate, she was assigned to provide administrative support to the Section Chief of the Advocacy Department. The role allowed her to closely observe her female boss who possessed many strengths that Rehnuma would come to admire in a leader...one of which was being open to new ideas from anyone, regardless of rank.

During an offsite leadership retreat—emboldened with the knowledge that her boss was receptive to new ideas—Rehnuma raised her hand and pitched the idea of holding a

Youth Forum in Bangladesh. This had never been done before and what made the idea even more special was Rehnuma's suggestion that children of all income levels be included, and that the children themselves help design the forum. Her boss loved the idea; so did the other leaders at the retreat.

The forum was a great success and received a lot of media attention. The most powerful moment of the forum was when representatives from the highest levels of government eagerly listened when the children presented solutions to existing problems.

Based on her own life experiences, Rehnuma strongly believes that our lives are made up of the choices we make. She believes, too, that young people all over the world are often shortsighted about the lifelong impacts that bad choices can have. Conversely, given the right opportunity, mentoring, and tools, children can make better decisions while applying their unique gifts to make meaningful contributions to the world. She says that everyone has agency. Everyone can make a difference in some small way.

Rehnuma went on to get her PhD from Penn State University, and later joined the State University of New York (SUNY) at Brockport as a faculty member, teaching a course on nonprofit management. In the same way that she had involved the children in the design of the Youth Leadership Forum, she asked her students to develop an idea for a nonprofit that could contribute to empowering young people. After careful consideration and a lot of hard work, they launched "Heroes for All." The organization's mission is to help young people find the hero within and then become a hero for others. The organization is officially registered in the United States as a 501(c)3, and also in Bangladesh under the Social Welfare act, and it develops initiatives to help young people activate their potential and build themselves as conscious global citi-

> Leading since 2017
>
> **Rehnuma Karim, PhD**
> *CEO and founder of Heroes for All*
>
> As a leader, you'll get the most joy out of working with committed colleagues to better the lives of those who would most benefit from thoughtful care, attention, and love. The initiatives of Heroes for All are focused on letting people know that everyone matters, and that they too can do great things in the world with their own unique gifts. Touching people's lives is the most rewarding part of leading.

zens. To date, Heroes for All has done such things as organize leadership seminars for inner-city youth in the US, start a cross-cultural program to help children in the US and Bangladesh overcome stereotypes and biases, distribute groceries to more than three thousand households in Bangladesh during the Covid lockdowns, build a school for underprivileged children on the outskirts of the capital of Bangladesh, and launch Camp Abilities, a first-of-its-kind four-day sports camp for children with visual impairments.

Rehnuma isn't the kind of leader who is satisfied with just a compelling vision. Her real satisfaction comes in converting that vision into true and lasting differences in people's lives. Witnessing first-hand the positive impact that Heroes for All is making, Rehnuma left academia and now dedicates her time to advancing Heroes for All as the nonprofit's CEO. Wild girl? Nah. She's a leader who gets results!

FINISH COMPLETELY

My company once hired a social media marketing firm that, for the purposes of this story, I'll call Future Plans. The firm was run by a creative guy named Caleb (another alias). My company wanted to bring more exposure to all our services and our impressive client list. Caleb was quite talented at identifying market trends and thinking of (or up) clever means of showcasing my company's services. He would frequently say, "What we could do is..." After leaving meetings where he had offered sound ideas, I would feel encouraged that we were headed in the right direction and psyched up about the plans we had developed, and then nothing would happen! I'd have to send Caleb multiple follow-up emails to get updates, and often he'd have plausible excuses about why the work was progressing at the pace of a psychedelically tranquilized snail. I got so frustrated that I reached out to a friend who also had done work with Caleb and Future Plans to hear about his experiences. My friend relayed a similar experience: Caleb would get his company all fired up with ideas, and then nothing would happen. My friend and I agreed that we wished Caleb had named his company Future Results, not Future Plans. What use is a plan that doesn't result in anything, right?

I came within inches of terminating our agreement with Caleb and his company. Fortunately, Courtenay, his more detail- and task-oriented project manager, took charge of our account. She made things happen and led many effective marketing initiatives for my company. A few years later, Caleb closed his business to become the marketing director with a larger firm. My company quickly signed a new agreement with Courtenay, which was an easy decision, as by then she had established a reliable track record of results.

When you're a leader, you don't have to do the doing, but you do have to get the doing done. It's fine to be a thinker, conceptualizer, planner, or "creative type," as long as you've got somebody who can convert your thoughts into tangible actions and results. As a leader, you will quickly find that getting results often requires helping others get results on your behalf. Doing so adds additional strands of horsehair to the sword dangling above your head.

MO' BETTER

The word "result" implies a finished outcome. Sometimes, though, there won't be an end, per se. Some initiatives you lead will be ongoing, yet will still be a reflection of your ability to make things happen. In these instances, the aim is to persistently enhance whatever purposes and/or outcomes the initiative was designed to advance. Results, in these instances, are continuously perfecting something through ongoing incremental refinements and improvements, doing Mo' Better.

When you're a leader, you don't have to do the doing, but you do have to get the doing done.

In mid-2007, I was asked to co-develop, design, and deliver an eighteeen-month leadership development program for The Walsh Group, a Chicago-based construction company. Founded in 1898, the company wanted to develop a leadership enhancement program for up-and-coming leaders. The program officially launched in December 2007 and has become a leader preparation program staple in the years since. Called the Walsh Group Leadership Initiative (WGLI), each iteration of the program has a cohort of 30 emerging leaders attending ten "summits," each focused on a critical leadership-related topic (e.g., leading culture, change, teams, risk). Each attendee also completes various surveys to better understand their motivators, stressors, and productive and counterproductive leadership behaviors. Each attendee also gets one-on-one leadership coaching to help personalize their experience within the program. Adding oomph to the program is the fact that joining the cohort for each summit are the company's most senior leaders. Often those execs are involved in teaching content segments or leading breakout discussions. Being there also allows those execs to see the next generation of leaders in action.

During the program, cohort members are also divided into Strategic Action Teams (SAT) and tasked with working on an issue of business importance and presenting their best recommendations to the company's leadership near the end of the WGLI program. The SATs not only help teach important skills for leaders working with other leaders, but the teams also help the company derive an immediate return on their investment in the program, instead of having to wait until each leader "graduates," applies what they have learned, and starts achieving more substantial results for the company.

In their book *Learning Leadership,* famed leadership researchers Jim Kouzes and Barry Posner say that leaders need to constantly ask a two-word question: What's better? Whatever results you've achieved today need to be exceeded tomorrow. Leaders can, and should, celebrate milestones and achievements. But they should never quite be fully satisfied. In that spirit, though the WGLI program is now over a decade old, and over 150 leaders have gone through the program during seven eighteen-month iterations; we continue to refine, enhance, and improve the program. Periodically throughout each WGLI program, I get together with Roy Epps, the program's executive sponsor and one of the company presidents, and Craig Atkinson, the program's codeveloper. We call our get togethers "Design Days"—and we discuss the impact of prior summits while planning for the summits ahead. The focus is always on making the program more powerful, transformative, educational, and impactful. Bear in mind, we don't have to do this. The program is wired. We could put it on autopilot and it would still be good. But we see it as our responsibility to continue to make the program the best it can be, and then, when we've gotten it to that point, make it better still. That keeps the three of us sharp and engaged. We agreed that we never wanted to be like the aged university professor who lost his passion years ago and still refers to ancient notes that have never been upgraded. Nope, we made a pact to never become stale and predictable. We'd rather take what works and make the results Mo' Better!

MARATHON RESULTS

Results rarely come instantly or easily, and eking out more becomes harder as you advance in your leadership influence and rank. Before you become a leader, you can knock items off your to-do list rapidly. Then you become a leader and tasks are bigger and more complex, involving more people and more shaping. In the senior ranks, you might be involved in shaping a strategic decision that takes years of upfront data gathering, discussing, and evaluating, and more years to implement and refine before reaping the result you want. Executive decisions such as whether to launch new products or services, develop new markets, upgrade systems and technologies, or expand geographically, impact the entire enterprise and thus must be done thoughtfully and carefully. I once worked on a corporate succession plan that culminated in a CEO transition that took a full ten years. It took additional years for the CEO to fully acclimate to his new role.

One company owner with whom I work is fond of reminding his employees that the company is in it for the long game, and that business is a marathon, not a sprint. As a new leader, you may sometimes feel like you have to accomplish everything as quickly as humanly possible. Working with urgency is good, working with fury is not. Yes, over and over again, you're going to have to deliver the goods, make real things happen, and move the organization forward through your work. Since getting results will be an ever-present part of your job, why not just make it part of your regular routine? Plan—work—finish. Repeat.

THINK NOW/*ACT NOW*

Think Now

What is an example of something you helped "make happen" that contributed to your bosses putting you into a leadership role? If you don't know, ask. What you learn might surprise you.

Do you feel a sense of pressure to get results? Describe why you feel that way.

Some results take a long time to achieve. Describe a significant result you made happen that took you six months or longer to achieve. What did you learn from this experience?

What is a substantial task or initiative you're working on that doesn't have a definite ending, but where ongoing improvements are expected?

Act Now

- List some exceptional results you would like to achieve in your work role in the next year. For each result, identify one specific action you could take to increase the likelihood of the result happening. Also consider including other go-getters who could help you make those results happen.
- Sit down with your boss and review the exceptional results list you just identified. Get their enhancements/additions/edits to the list.
- Identify one work task that you haven't gotten around to finishing and finish it.
- Take a look at Heroes for All and consider donating! Heroes-forall.org

BONUS TIP

Getting results, like so many other leadership-related responsibilities, takes discipline. More important than the volume of results you get will be the quality. Better to finish a stellar job than a half-assed one. A lot of new leaders say "yes" to every request and then set out to get it all done by themselves. Don't. It's a sign of immature leadership. Conversely, setting workload boundaries is a sign of leadership maturity. Putting in the disciplined effort to achieve exceptional results often necessitates scuttling or postponing some item of lesser importance.

Setting boundaries takes courage. Specifically, the courage to push back when you're assigned unrealistic workloads or deadlines, and the courage to voice a strong, assertive, and hopefully infrequent "No!" In my company's courage-building workshops we talk about the importance of judiciously asserting boundaries by having the courage to say "No!" Learn to apply this kind of courage.

Your two-word bonus tip is what we call

"NO" COURAGE

CHAPTER 13

MASTER MANAGEMENT

Apply Fundamentals to Have More Impact

Many leadership books have covered the difference between leadership and management, with the former being visionary and strategic, and the latter being tactical and operational. While it's true the two aren't exactly the same, there are a lot of complementarities and overlaps between them. Both involve advancing goals, improving performance, mitigating risk, making sound decisions, behaving ethically and professionally, understanding human motivation, and developing people. There's so much overlap that it sometimes feels like management is just a less intense version of leadership.

This chapter focuses on all the management stuff that surrounds leadership—the stuff you can't neglect, and if you learn to master it, it will greatly improve your effectiveness and impact as a leader. There's a good chance the organization you work for provides some form of basic management training. Even if they don't, there are thousands of easily obtainable books on the subject. Thus, in this chapter, we focus at a high level on those management essentials that, if you master them, will make you a better leader. In the same way a springboard diver or figure skater needs to be adept in the compulsory acrobatic moves, good leaders need to be proficient in the foundational aspects of management.

GOAL GETTING

Human beings are goal-directed creatures. Goals give us a destination that we can move toward and a means to gauge our progress as we go. Even before we learn to set goals for ourselves, others are setting them for us. With the goal of getting us to talk, our parents repeat words over and over until we start saying them ourselves. They keep pushing us along with other little goals (e.g., dressing ourselves, learning manners, riding a bike, wiping our hiney) toward the greater goal of turning us into self-reliant and capable young adults who can eventually face the world on our own. This goal-directed journey to self-sufficiency is aided and reinforced by relatives, teachers, sports coaches, and countless others until the whole notion of goals and advancement is wired into our being.

Good management starts with clear goals. Goals give people a sense of momentum, confirming that each day they and the organization are moving forward. Progress toward goals is the clearest way of knowing that what you're doing at work truly matters and that you're making a positive difference.

Before you set individual performance goals for each team member, you need to work with the team to establish unified team goals. The important thing is that the goals of the team you're leading link to the goals of the department or division your team is a part of. Likewise, the division's goals should connect with the business unit's goals, and on up the line until all the goals of each team in the enterprise, in some way, fit into the strategic goals that are driving the entire organization. The linkage is important. Many studies confirm that the lower you go into an organization, the less likely people are to be aware of what top-level goals are driving the organization. Don't let that be you. If you—and by extension your team—don't know what your organization's strategic priorities are, go ask your boss. Quickly.

BS GOALS

It's striking how many organizations have vague goals that are really nothing more than platitudes. Soooo many business owners cite their company's biggest goal as "make more money than last year." Duh. Obviously! Like, do they think that everyone is going to catch a brain-shrinking virus and suddenly become dumb to the fact that the organization needs to grow?! You laugh, but here are some actual bullshit "goals" I've heard communicated in companies:

- Be more competitive.
- Provide more leadership.
- Reduce expenses.
- Increase customer focus.
- Do better.
- Communicate more!

I mean, come on. Really? Those aren't goals, those are ongoing business imperatives. To have any chance of motivating people and moving the organization forward, goals must be clear, measurable, reachable, and set against a realistic deadline. Here are some better examples from my clients:

- Reduce year-over-year employee turnover by 10 percent by the end of this year.
- Lower company overhead expenses by 3 percent by the end of the third quarter this year.
- Increase employee engagement by 7 percent, as measured by the company's annual employee engagement survey, by December 31.

You get the idea. As you and your team collaborate to set clear goals, it also helps to take each individual goal and add additional context and reasoning to it. Doing so makes the goal more explicit and helps make it actionable. Here's a set of questions you can use to add dimension to goals:

- Why is this goal important to the team? What positive changes will result from satisfying this goal?
- How will achieving this goal help advance the strategic goals of our department, division, and/or company?
- What measures can we use to track our progress or lack thereof?
- What resources (time, money, people, sponsorship) will we need to successfully do the work?
- What factors could hinder our ability to achieve the goal? How can we mitigate those risks?
- What initial actions need to be taken, who should be assigned the action, and when does the action need to be completed?

The important thing is that you tee up your goals in a way that they're more likely to get done. Goal setting is only useful to the extent that it results in goal getting!

GULP GOALS

Once you've set team goals, you have to set individual team member goals that connect to them. The most motivational performance goals, in my opinion, are those that simultaneously frighten and excite. I call these Gulp Goals—when you realize what's being asked of you, you swallow hard and go, Gulp! Goals like this shouldn't arise unilaterally from you. Rather, they should be identified through thoughtful individual conversations with each person you lead. They should stem from and build upon already achieved goals and skills that both of you agree would be in the person's best interest to develop. They will be far more likely to stretch toward goals if they shaped them. The opposite is also true: they'll practically stand still if they feel like you've unilaterally decided the goal you want them to chase.

Goal setting is only useful to the extent that it results in goal getting.

You don't want to have goals become like New Year's Resolutions that quickly recede in importance. Leadership, as covered in the last chapter, is about results, right? Here are some ways of ensuring that the goals you and your direct reports set will be achieved:

- Write them down, explicitly and clearly. Include how the goal fits into the broader team and organizational goals to clarify the linkage between their goals and the organization's broader aims. Doing so makes their work important.
- Write down the risks that could emerge if the goal isn't attained (e.g., Clarify Consequences) and the rewards for exceeding the goal.
- Identify measures that will be reviewed to gauge and track goal progress.
- Identify the resources, training, or support that the person will be given to help them advance the goal, including whatever specific help you, as the leader, will provide.
- Set a realistic but aggressive deadline to create urgency. Also, set Momentum Milestones and dates

when the two of you will meet to evaluate the progress toward the goals. These periodic check-ins are key to promoting accountability.

As with the team goals, when you set individual goals it's critical to drive out any vagueness. Instead of a silly goal like "communicate more" say, "We agree you will lead our bi-weekly staff meetings, and immediately afterward you and I will jointly evaluate the meeting's effectiveness on a scale ranging from 'highly ineffective' to 'highly effective.'" You get the idea. The more specific the goal, the better the chances the goal will be reached.

PRIORITIZE PRIORITIES

In chapter 4 you learned that mastering time is essential to gaining personal control. In the same way, as a leader, you'll gain control over the work to the extent that you thoughtfully prioritize all the priorities you and your team must respond to. All things being equal, not all things are equal. Meaning, not all tasks and deliverables have the same importance or urgency. Some work just matters more. And, if you approach all tasks with equal urgency, the ones that warrant the most attention may suffer; important items become trivialized and trivial items become important. As a leader, you need to work with your team to prioritize priorities so that it can distinguish between trivial and important.

Dr. Stephen Covey warned that too many people get caught up in the thick of thin things, and when it comes to priorities, he said, "The main thing is to keep the main thing the main thing." Amid the daily grind, it's normal to get focused on the little tasks in front of us, punching out our "to do" lists, losing sight of our team's larger purpose and the more important work that advances it. Layer on unexpected

Leading since 1996

Ahli Moore

President, X-Factor Solutions

I was once part of a consulting team that was on an engagement for a large telecom company. The company would frequently refer to its 'corporate priority list.' When we asked how many corporate priorities there were, they answered, '150.' Let me tell you something. If you have 150 priorities, you don't have any priorities. The company was bought out within a few years.

emergencies often caused by another team's lack of planning or prioritizing, and before you know it, you and your team are so far afield from your priorities that you've lost sight of what's important and are no longer making progress.

All things being equal, not all things are equal.

Prioritizing priorities is one of the management responsibilities that leaders need to master. After getting some initial direction from your boss, make a list to identify the most dramatic goals and priorities first, and then list the rest in relative order underneath. For example, at the request of the director of safety for one of my clients, I facilitated a strategic visioning session focused on the department's three-year-ahead priorities. The safety director suggested we start by prioritizing the STCKY stuff. When I asked him what that meant, he replied "Stuff That Can Kill You." Except he used a stronger word than "stuff."

While your team's priorities might not involve deadly consequences, they are likely dramatic in some other way. You may find it helpful to identify the criteria you'll use to gauge priorities, such as the impact on safety, finances, customers, workload, performance, morale, risk, and operations. You could even go a step further and weight each criterion in terms of importance so that you can objectively prioritize them. Regardless of which method you use, the important thing is to prioritize priorities, and then review them with your boss and team.

EXPECT / INSPECT

Goal setting and prioritizing are two ways of clarifying what's expected of each person you're leading, and one of the primary management responsibilities you'll need to master. It's important for people to know how their individual efforts contribute to the broader goals and priorities of the overall organization. There will, of course, be other expectations that you'll need to communicate. Everyone also needs to know...

- why the work of your team(s) is important to the organization.
- where the team(s) resides on the org chart, and how it fits in the overall enterprise.
- the expectations those outside your team(s), such as leaders and/or other teams that rely on your team's work, have of your team.
- standards of performance that everyone is expected to abide by.
- standards with regulations, such as those related to safety, or preventing sexual harassment or bullying.

Clarifying expectations will never stop being an essential part of your job. But it's not enough to communicate expectations. A lot of rookie leaders state their expectations and then are shocked and frustrated when their people only partially meet the expectations or fail to meet them altogether.

Leading since 2008

Olga Ivanova

American Councils for International Education

True leaders communicate realistic and clear expectations, which makes performing the work easier and more rewarding. They also provide instant feedback, good or bad, which provides even more clarity, inspiration, and learning. The best leaders set expectations, let you know whether you're meeting them, and keep you motivated to improve!

That frustration would be better directed at the rookie leaders themselves. In clarifying expectations, they only did half their job.

Along with setting clear expectations, you've got to stay apprised of the progress your team is making toward them. As one vice president whom I've coached for a long time said, "It took me a while to realize that you've got to check in with people to see where they are. Before I learned that, I would pull my hair out when people didn't follow through on commitments we had agreed upon. I didn't get how they didn't get it! Then I started having weekly check-ins with each of my reports, and we'd review how well they were meeting those expectations. Knowing they were going to have to provide weekly updates amped up the accountability. Two words that I keep in the forefront of my mind are expect and inspect."

A lot of justifiable emphasis has been placed on the dangers of micromanagement. No one likes to work under a microscope, having their every move scrutinized and evaluated. Raise your hand if you absolutely loved being controlled by someone else. I didn't think so.

While micromanagement is bad, so is an abdication of management! Inspecting people's work and progress isn't micromanagement…it's just management. It's part of your job. No, you don't have to inspect work like an interrogating prosecutor, and no, you don't have to monitor progress with the frequency of a bleeping electrocardiogram machine. But you do have to monitor and inspect people's work regularly. Of course, you can and should do so in a supportive and empowering way. You're staying updated on their progress, not to catch them doing things wrong so you can punish them but to stay involved with their work and offer whatever support and guidance you can to help them be successful.

MAKE MONEY

In business and in life, people seem to fit into two broad categories: Spenders and Savers. As a leader, you can't afford to be financially oblivious—unaware of what your team spends or takes in, or how it helps the company generate more revenue or spend less money. Particularly in owner-led companies, it's common to hear the phrase, "Act like an owner." What this generally means is:

- Take as much interest in the financial health of the organization as the owners do.
- Be frugal and don't spend money on stupid stuff.
- Know all the impacts your team has on profits or savings.
- Always make or save more money.

Not all leaders are in functions that directly impact paying customers. Leaders, for example, who lead internal or administrative teams don't bring in dollars for the company. But you and your team still impact profitability with the overhead costs you cause the business to incur. Especially in these instances, you as a leader need to understand the value that your team or area provides to the business. One way to do this is to consider what would our business lose if our function were gone tomorrow?

Drawing on the earlier safety team example, how might it go about justifying the money it costs the business? Objectively, the entire department is a significant cost to the business. The safety standards the entire company must comply with, along with all necessary safety equipment, incur plenty of costs. But what if the company did away with your department? Eliminating the costs would result in far bigger expenses. Hospitalization costs, insurance costs, and legal costs would all skyrocket. So would the company's reputational costs as many within the organization would start looking for employment in safer settings. Talk about STCKY!

The challenge is that when you and your team aren't in a revenue-generating role, it's easy for outsiders to question the value that you provide or the costs that you incur. It becomes your responsibility to clarify, justify, and communicate that value. Even if your team is a cost to the business, you need to show how your team or area makes the company money by being far less expensive than the result if the team were eliminated. Always make money!

DEFINITELY RTFCA

Most sizable organizations have a legal or contract management function. Nearly all organizations that provide goods or services have signed agreements in place specifying the terms under which those goods and services will be provided. If you work in such a place, and if you're in a leadership role, you've got to become knowledgeable about those contract terms. This is especially true if the work your team does is, in fact, operating under some type of contractual obligation.

Too many inexperienced leaders get burned because they didn't carefully read or understand contract terms. And, contracts do more than specify terms. They clarify risks and offer protection. Since they are most often written by lawyers, they are filled with mind-numbing legalese. The lawyers who write the contracts are only interested in protecting the company they work for and shifting away as much of the risk as possible. If you're not careful, and you sign an agreement that puts you or your organization on the hook for something it can't deliver, you can do a lot of financial and reputational harm to your organization.

A longtime lawyer in the legal department for one of my clients keeps a bat in the corner of his office with the letters RTFCA burned into the wood. These same letters are on his car's personalized license plate. He works in a company where project managers deliver major work projects for large client entities and all those projects are governed by contracts. If the project teams don't deliver on time and within budget, there are often "liquidated damages"—financial penalties often approaching tens of thousands of dollars. Having seen his company burned by lackadaisical project managers who didn't read the contract too many times to count, he decided to showcase **RTFCA** as his personal mantra, reflecting the imperative that all managers **R**ead **T**he **F**-ing **C**ontract...**A**gain!

BASIC MANAGEMENT

There are five broad, widely accepted functions that constitute great management. Four are explained below. The fifth—leading—is the focus of this book.

Planning: Involves forecasting the future, setting goals and strategies, establishing performance standards, identifying necessary resources, and pinpointing and prioritizing the right tactics and actions to further the goals and strategies.

Organizing: Setting the right structure to support the overall plans and work, establishing and coordinating roles and responsibilities, allocating resources based on planned priorities, and clarifying the boundaries of decision authority within and among the roles.

Staffing: Attracting, recruiting, developing, evaluating, and rewarding and compensating talent.

Controlling: Monitoring, evaluating, and measuring progress toward plans and goals, taking corrective action as needed, continuously improving performance, and putting processes and procedures in place that support safety, production, reporting, and decision-making.

If you really want to Master Management, you must first master the basics!

THINK NOW/*ACT NOW*

Think Now

Have you and your team written down your goals? Be honest. Most people and teams haven't. If you have, good for you! Having read this chapter, how might your goals be improved?

Think back to a significant achievement you accomplished at work. Was it the result of a goal or goals? How was your level of motivation impacted by the goal?

What are the most significant goals that you and your team are pursuing in the year ahead? Are you making adequate progress? How do you know?

What are your organization's top strategic goals? How do your team's goals contribute to advancing them? How do the goals of each individual on your team contribute to advancing the team's goals?

Act Now

- Write down your goals.
- Work with your team to write down the team's goals.

- If you don't know your organization's top strategic goals, go find out what they are. Then inform your team.
- Drawing upon the team's goals, prioritize the team's priorities.
- Set calendar dates and times for inspecting progress toward team and individual goals and priorities.
- If the work your team does is related in any way to your company's contractual obligations, read that contract. Then read it again. Then educate your team about it. Definitely RTFCA!

BONUS TIP

One of the oldest tools in the management archives is SWOT Analysis. It's a management staple. You and your team can use it across a range of applications. A SWOT can be used to evaluate such things as the team itself, major initiatives the team is driving, or work the team is considering taking on. Most often it's used as a tool during the strategic planning process. It uses four quadrants—Strengths, Weaknesses, Opportunities, and Threats... hence SWOT, which can be represented on paper with a 2 x 2 quadrant matrix, or by using four pieces of flipchart paper.

Strengths: What are we doing particularly well?

Weaknesses: What do we need to do better?

Opportunities: What could we exploit or take advantage of?

Threats: what could severely hinder our progress?

Strengths and opportunities are those things that advance progress, and weaknesses and threats are those that hinder progress. Generally, strengths and weaknesses are considered internal attributes, such as strengths or weaknesses of the team itself, and opportunities and threats are considered external conditions that could help or hinder the team.

Your two-word bonus tip is:

SWOT STUFF

CHAPTER 14

LEAD UP

Succeed by Supporting Your Boss's Success

Your individual leadership success is contingent upon you making others successful. While you want to have a positive influence on everyone you touch through your leadership work, your leadership fate will be mostly determined by your influence over the success of the people you lead—which you read about in part two—and how successful you help your boss become. This chapter focuses on learning to lead the leaders who lead you.

Quite a lot has been written about how to "manage up." Much of it is common sense; do a good job, support the boss's goals, communicate, follow through, and deliver results. Honestly, though, shouldn't ALL employees do those things, not just those in management roles? I prefer the term "leading up," and I see the practices as quite distinct from the everyday behaviors that we should expect of all workers. Leading up involves doing certain things that inspire your bosses to take actions, shift their thinking, or make decisions that they otherwise wouldn't have without your influence.

Leading your leaders is the clearest way of proving that you are ready to take on more responsibility. It's also a way of making a real difference in your organization. I've seen entire initiatives and programs spawned by passionate but inexperienced leaders because they were able to successfully draw the interest and attention of more senior leaders who believed in their cause. For example, one team of new leaders met for months researching the topic of diversity, equity, and inclusion. They had tough and honest conversations about whether the company was doing enough to recruit and develop underrepresented minority groups, and if not, whether and how to amp up those efforts. Then they put together a business case, which included the strong rationale that the business's own customers were more diverse than the company, and that more aggressive recruiting would broaden the talent pool available to the company, creating a competitive advantage. Everything culminated in a well-practiced presentation to the young leaders' very non-diverse bosses. As a result, the company did, in fact, intensify its recruiting of minority populations. It also, for the first time, assigned a person to lead the company's DEI efforts. Then the senior leaders, inspired by the younger leaders' leadership, put out a declarative pledge to create a culture of care that is "diverse, safe, welcoming, and inclusive." Sometimes the most important company changes come from leaders below the senior-leader ranks who are brave enough to lead up.

BE UBIQUITOUS

You'll have more influence if you and the differences you're making are visible. New leaders sometimes become insular, focused only on the tasks and challenges right in front of them. It's fine to be a hands-on, heads-down workhorse… if you make a point of regularly involving yourself in other things outside of your team, lifting your head up to stay involved with the broader organization. Most organizations have plenty of avenues for applying and showcasing your leadership influence. Join ad hoc committees. Get involved with recruiting on college campuses. Interview new-hire prospects. Participate as a facilitator in training those at lower levels. Join the company's softball team. Volunteer to organize the company's annual 10K fundraiser. Seriously, there's no shortage of ways to get involved.

The point is for you to become a fully immersed and well-rounded corporate citizen. Doing so broadens your network, helps you develop more meaningful bonds with the people you work with, deepens your loyalty and company pride, and gives your leadership additional exposure. The more your positive involvement is noticed, the more you are noticed. The old saying, "It's who you know, not what you know that matters" is only partially true. It's not just who you know that matters, but who knows you. Being a good corporate citizen raises your leadership visibility and profile by helping you become known.

For many years, one of my clients, Aldridge Electric Inc., has been involved with Bridges to Prosperity, a U.S.-based nonprofit that partners with foreign governments to build pedestrian bridges in remote places. It turns out that rural isolation is a root cause of poverty, and simply building pedestrian bridges, such as those required to walk over dangerous rivers, can help more indigenous people enter the labor market and have greater access to healthcare and economic opportunity. Under the leadership of Amy Bang, Bridge to Prosperity's CEO, some 350 trail bridges have been built throughout the world. Aldridge employees from all levels eagerly compete in a fundraiser to earn the right to join a bridge-building expedition team. The folks who raise the most money, regardless of level, get to be part of the expedition.

The work is incredibly meaningful and incredibly grueling. Crews work from early morning until sunset in beautiful but sweltering locations that are full of mosquitoes, oversized bugs, and exotic snakes. At night, the crews sleep under noisy jungle canopies in primitive camps. The entire experience is full of mud, sweat, and exhaustion. But it's also full of genuine camaraderie, complete with campfire songs, storytelling, and homecooked meals prepared by the villagers. Yes, it's hard, but it's made less so because they're all in it together.

One of the interesting aspects of the work is that the crews don't retain whatever leadership rank they held back at Aldridge's headquarters. Crew members have included a company president, an executive vice president, numerous vice presidents, field superintendents, and those in non-management roles such as administrative assistants. But while on the crews, those titles are left behind. The work itself, combined with natural talents, drives who takes on what role. Today you might be carrying rocks or pouring a concrete foundation, tomorrow you might be pulling cable or hammering wood. Removing the company's traditional hierarchy reveals people in a new light. The boss whom you might have found intimidating back at work turns out to be a great camp organizer. Likewise, the quiet estimator whom people trust with spreadsheets in the office can also be trusted to do manual labor for hours and hours without complaint. Beyond the charitable benefits of the experience is the benefit of getting to work with people in a new way and learning to see them in a new light. People who are sometimes overlooked as "role players" back at the office come to be seen as essential leaders without whom the bridge-building project would have been diminished and less enjoyable.

Involving yourself in charitable and other outside-of-work activities is a great way to further apply your leadership influence, contribute to the greater good, demonstrate your loyalty to your company, and get noticed by other involved leaders!

EXPERIENCE GAP

The gap between what seasoned leaders need from less experienced leaders and what they get is vast. The more desperate you are to impress your leaders or the more starstruck you are in their presence, the bigger the gap will be.

Your confidence as a new leader will grow as you become more competent. Until then, do your best not to be hesitant around your leaders, or intimidated by their titles. Show inner strength by doing the following:

Speak Truthfully: Your leaders need to know the fullness of the situation you're presenting to them. There's no need to sugarcoat things, and if you do, you'll do more harm than good. Think, "What would I want to know if I had to deal with this situation?" and then tell them those things. The more truthful you are, the more you will be trusted and relied upon by your boss. That's the essence of Leading Up.

Early Warnings: This connects to what you learned in the introduction about "No Surprises." Don't play the hero, thinking that you'll be able to solve every issue without the input and help of your leaders. If you're too afraid to ask for help, you're too afraid.

Good Alternatives: Yes, there are many problems you'll encounter as a young leader that are "above your pay grade" to solve or resolve. But never allow a complex challenge be your excuse to wuss out from at least offering your best thinking. When you bring an issue or problem to your boss, also come with your best thinking, and say, "I was thinking we might address it like this..."

Accessible Details: It makes sense that you want to prepare and understand every tiny detail when you're queried about an issue and called into your boss's office. You definitely want to know all the details, so beat up that spreadsheet every which way you can. But for goodness' sake, don't start reviewing that spreadsheet item by item and explaining every formula you used to create it. Let your boss direct how much detail to provide but have it all at the ready in case they want more.

Calm Confidence: Yep, your boss can negatively impact your career. Yep, they have a ton more experience than you and that's intimidating. Lose the self-consciousness; it just makes you look weak. Instead, view every opportunity to present to your boss as a chance to impress them. Show them that you give a rip and that you are as eager to resolve the issue as they are and that you've got some ideas for doing just that.

THINK FORWARD

You're not just paid to do a job. You're paid to think and to apply that thinking in a way that moves the organization forward. One of the breakout activities I like to do with groups is ask them to flipchart the difference between a good employee and a great one. Answers often include: great employees "go the extra mile," "go above-and-beyond," and "do whatever it takes." All of these are true, of course, but there's another difference that may not be obvious: they're not afraid to offer ideas.

As a new leader, you may think that the leaders above you have everything under control and if they want your ideas, they'll ask for them. You'd be surprised how eager your leaders are for fresh and new ways of doing things, especially if those ideas further the leader's goals, or create efficiencies that help the organization make or save money. Your leaders often know less than you give them credit for, and they are hungry for your forward-moving ideas. Providing them, thoughtfully, respectfully, and boldly will help your leadership career.

This may seem strange, but one of the most productive things a leader can do is get away from all his or her work interruptions (typically away from the workplace) and think forward. One of the simplest definitions of the word lead is to "stay out in front," and you can't do that if you're always heads-down solving daily problems. You may feel self-conscious about spending an hour or two at a coffee house each week just so you can think forward, but that's what it takes to generate forward-moving ideas. So, identify a morning when the impact of your absence will be lightest, set aside an hour or two, use your favorite note-taking method, and for the good of your boss and the company, think forward!

You're not just paid to do a job. You're paid to think, and to apply that thinking in a way that moves the organization forward.

"But where do I start?" you may be thinking. "I can't just materialize a new idea out of a hat like a street magician." Good point. Here's an approach you may find more effective than sheer willpower: think beyond your boss's thinking. Be clear about the goals that are driving your boss, and what her thoughts are most often fixed on. Say, for example, your boss is intrigued by new technology and is weighing whether to adopt it in the department. Then you come across an online article that illustrates how another company was able to use the technology. You could just toss the article to your boss. But thinking beyond your boss's thinking might involve reaching out to the article's author and conversing with them about other applications for the technology and then connecting with other experts versed in the technology with whom the article's author might be willing to put you in touch. After speaking to those experts, you may surface additional ways the technology could impact your department, as well as some risks your boss wasn't aware of. On top of all that, now layer your own creative ideas and recommendations before bringing them to your boss. It will take an investment of time, sure, but probably less than a few hours. Will that legwork add value to the idea and be appreciated by your boss? Will your boss be impressed that you took the time to think beyond their thinking? Wouldn't you be if you were them?

When you think forward by thinking beyond your boss's thinking, you will go a long way toward ensuring that you will sit in your boss's seat someday.

ROUNDUP QUESTIONS

The biggest ideas involve multiple leaders, not just your boss. Transformational ideas often require the signoff of many leaders, so involving those leaders in shaping, scrutinizing, challenging, and championing ideas is important. When ideas are of the size and scale that multiple leaders and their areas will be affected, it is critical to go on a question roundup. The idea is to gather as many questions as possible so that you know what answers the leaders need to fully embrace the idea. In fact, the last question should be, "What else do you need to have answered correctly in order for you to fully support this idea?"

Too many inexperienced leaders spend hours putting together a detailed PowerPoint deck and start pitching answers they're hoping to get the other leaders to approve. They figure the idea will fly based solely on the strength of their own logic and intellect, neglecting the input of the other leaders whose approval and sponsorship they'll need. They bypass the questions and go right to the answers. Should it be a surprise when the leaders whose input was neglected give tepid support for the idea, if any?

When you think forward by thinking beyond your boss's thinking, you will go a long way toward ensuring that you will sit in your boss's seat someday.

Let's say, for example, your boss is the head of the facilities department, and she is seriously considering rearranging the work environment of one of the company's major business units from high-walled cubicles to low-walled, high-performance team (HPT) workstations. Her reasoning is that HPTs save money, require less maintenance, and promote creativity because employees can quickly communicate with one another, "huddling" as needed around a conference table that's set in the middle of the workspace. It's a good idea with very valid reasons for implementation. But if people just showed up to work one day and everyone's workspace had been rearranged, you know there would be holy hell to pay. Heads would roll!

In this scenario, to lead up you could approach your boss about going on a question roundup so that you could learn, firsthand, what objections other leaders have about the idea, and/or their ways of improving it. As part of the question roundup, after briefly introducing the idea during one-on-one interviews, you could ask:

- What are your initial impressions of the idea?
- Have you heard this idea before and have you had any experience with it?
- What initial concerns do you have about the idea, and what are your ideas for remedying them?
- What questions do you have about the idea that others likely have too?
- What refinements to the idea might make it even more attractive?
- What slight variations on this idea are also worth considering?
- If you were to prioritize your questions about the idea, what are the most critical?
- How might our competitors respond to this idea if we implement it?

- What else do you need to have answered correctly for you to fully support this idea?

A question roundup is a listening tour. By listening this way, you show other leaders that their input and clout matters while the idea itself gets shaped and often strengthened. When you unearth the questions that need to be answered, you are also by implication uncovering the vulnerabilities that need to be shored up before rolling out the idea. Finally, at the most practical level, by gathering all the questions that need to be answered, you're in a better position to draft FAQs, because if the people above you have a lot of questions, you can bet that the people below you will too.

Involving yourself this way as a young leader is another way of raising your profile. As you have one-on-one conversations about important ideas with leaders above you, they get introduced to your thinking, professionalism, company loyalty, and leadership.

ASK TWICE

Be forewarned, some leaders are instinctively "no" people. They meet every new idea, concept, or approach with folded-arms, a furrowed-brow, and a grouchy no!

Don't give up. Good ideas can withstand a lot of scrutiny and rejection. Some leaders are jaded or fossilized and thinking, "Yeah, we tried that twenty years ago and we had our butts handed to us. We don't need to do that again." When in fact doing that again often makes great sense because prior failed attempts can be used to light the way toward successful attempts in the future.

Rookie leaders sometimes crumble the first time a more senior leader grandstands with an intimidating no! It's important to remember that your boss's no doesn't always mean no. Rather, no often means, "I'm not yet convinced and I need more information before I can be persuaded." Other times the more senior leader may be testing you to see how much the idea really means to you, and how willing you are to fight for it. A "real" leader, they might think, will fight for what they believe is right. So, sometimes you just have to ask the senior leader, "Is your 'no' a forever-and-don't-ask-me-again 'no' or an I-need-more-information-and-I-give-you-permission-to-get-it 'no'?"

By the way, it's worth considering, too, whether you are an instinctively "no" person who has to be convinced of "yes." If so, be sure to inform the people you lead about the difference between a hard "no" and one that leaves greater room for exploring.

THINK NOW/*ACT NOW*

Think Now

What extracurricular work activities have you contributed to? What are some other ways you could be ubiquitous to become a more involved corporate citizen?

When was the last time you influenced the thinking of a more seasoned leader? In what ways did you think beyond their thinking?

How do you typically interact with leaders who outrank you? Referring to the Experience Gap image in this chapter, which "need versus want" gaps might you benefit from closing?

When was the last time a more senior person initially said "no" to one of your ideas, but you were eventually able to convince them to say "yes"?

When was the last time you said "no" to one of your direct report's ideas, but they were eventually able to convince you to say "yes"?

Is there an idea you pitched recently that received a no, but is worthy of pitching again?

Act Now

- Pick one company event that you would typically avoid that you know other leaders will be attending, and attend the event.
- Identify one work initiative that you or your boss are responsible for advancing. If the initiative involves other stakeholders or leaders in the company, use the roundup questions to gather the questions that need to be answered to secure their sponsorship.
- Get a pad of paper and a pen or your phone's notetaking app. Go to a coffee house during a workday for an hour or two and write down some ways that you could help advance one of your boss's goals. Think forward!
- Read this excellent article on managing up: themuse.com/advice/10-ways-to-get-your-boss-to-trust-you-completely.

BONUS TIP

There's a huge difference between leading up and being a suck-up. It's a sad fact that many employees see kissing-up to the boss as a way to win his or her favor. It may be common, but it's not very leader-like. Have some self-respect.

Get your boss's permission to be a truth-teller. In a disarmed moment, ask your boss whether they need you to be a yes-person to be successful in your role. Ninety-nine times out of one hundred they will say something like, "No! I need you to tell me what I need to know, not what you think I want to hear." When they tell you that, say, "Good. You have my promise that I'll tell it like it is, even when it's hard."

What you've now done is set a new relationship ground rule with your boss, one that allows you to communicate in a leader-like way. Then the next time you need to deliver a tough message to your boss, refer to the ground rule, "Hey boss, remember when we agreed that I would be truthful with you even when it's hard? Well, I have something hard to share..."

What's the two-word bonus tip related to leading up?

SPEAK TRUTHFULLY

Leadership Oath 3
A Promise to Do Great Work

I promise to be a good leader of the work to be done.

I promise to always remember that leadership is about producing real and impactful results, and the pressure to get those results is something I must accept as a leadership reality.

I will remain keenly aware of how the work I'm responsible for leading impacts revenues, expenses, and profits. Results for most workplaces equate to making money.

I will remember that good leadership, too, requires good management, and that setting and monitoring goals and priorities come with the territory.

I realize that a large portion of my leadership responsibilities have to do with advancing work safely, ethically, and responsibly. Thus,

I fully commit to doing a good job with the job that needs to be done!

Signed: ______________________________

Date: ______________________________

BE COURAGEOUS

There you have it. A lifetime of leadership advice jammed into one book. I hope the leader you are now is different from the leader who turned the first page. I also hope that you didn't just accept each idea or suggestion as gospel. Rather, I hope you involved yourself by doubting, resisting, challenging, and mentally chewing on the advice before adopting it as your own, or rejecting it for your own reasons.

I dedicated this book to you for a reason. There are a lot of people counting on you. Me included. We're counting on you to use your leadership influence to make the world a better place. We're counting on you to leave people better off than you found them. We're counting on you to do better than the leaders who came before you. Way back in the preface, I told you that you matter. And you do. A lot.

Stay in communion with your integrity and you'll do fine. Let your values direct your thoughts and actions. Be on guard against the ever-present temptation to lower your standards, mistreat people, and take advantage of your leadership advantages. Lots of leaders before you let the people who were counting on them down by doing those things. We're now counting on you to do better. We need you to.

I'll close the book with the same two words of advice that I shared in the book's dedication: *Be Courageous.* In the years ahead, you'll face tough times, big challenges, and complicated people. Every leader does. Keep doing the next right thing, especially when doing the wrong thing is easier. Face your fears, help others face theirs, and take action. Put your leadership to good use by being a good leader.

I believe in you. Lots of other people believe in you too. I hope that you believe in yourself more now too. I'm proud of you for picking up this book and wanting to become a better leader. I'm grateful for the trust you put in me, and for the positive impact I know you'll make in the world. Now go out there and get to work. Just remember to take things two words at a time!

DISCUSSION GUIDE

Introduction What attracts you to leadership and what qualities do you have that you feel will make you a competent and effective leader? Who do you know that exhibits these qualities as a leader?

Chapter 1 What values or principles helped make possible the achievement you are most proud of? Is there a time when you failed to live those values or principles? What was the effect of that lapse?

Chapter 2 What positive impact do you hope to have on others through your leadership influence? Why is having this impact important to you?

Chapter 3 Who is someone you consider to have a great work ethic? What elements of their work ethic do you share? Do they do something you want to emulate?

Chapter 4 What did you envision the role of a leader to be before you started your current position? How does that vision compare with the reality you have experienced so far?

Chapter 5 What are some subtle ways that people have begun treating you differently or special since you've moved into your leadership role? If you let your ego get carried away with that special treatment, how might it change you? What actions can you take to ensure that you keep that special treatment in perspective?

Chapter 6 How would you characterize your degree of spiritual fitness? Are you in healthy spiritual shape? If not, what is the most important thing you need to address?

Chapter 7 As a leader, what do you view as the risks associated with trusting your direct reports? What are the risks associated with not trusting them?

Chapter 8 Have you ever used fear to motivate people to start or stop doing something? How did the fear impact the results you did or didn't achieve? How did the fear impact your relationship with the people you were en*fear*ing?

Chapter 9 What has been your experience with delegating thus far? How might it benefit you to delegate more? How could you use delegation to develop the people you're leading?

Chapter 10 What beliefs do you hold about racism and prejudice? How might those beliefs impact your leadership and your influence on those you're leading?

Chapter 11 What are some pleasant and rewarding aspects of your managerial position and are there ways you can make them even better?

Chapter 12 Do you feel a sense of pressure to get results? Describe why you feel that way. What are some ways that you can you manage the pressure?

Chapter 13 Write down your goals and your team's goals. How do they work together?

Chapter 14 How do you typically interact with leaders who outrank you? Does this influence your interactions with your direct reports?

ACKNOWLEDGMENTS

I'm not one to write "on spec." I only write when I'm moved to do so. Years can go by before the spirit moves me to write. I don't know where that spirit comes from or what it is. I just know that when I'm in writing mode, that spirit and I spend a lot of intimate time together, and, ever-so-briefly, it opens me to the joyful experience of creative flow. Thank you, great spirit, for guiding my way.

Special thanks are due to training legend Elaine Biech, for writing such an inviting foreword. I'm also grateful to the many luminary endorsers who gave the book their seal of approval. Writing a book is often likened to birthing a child. Your endorsements are like gifts at a baby shower celebration. The book and I are grateful for the gift of your well-wishes.

The good folks at Berrett-Koehler Publishers have been enthusiastic supporters of my work since publishing my first book, *Right Risk*, in 2003. Your coaching, guidance, and candid feedback always make for a better book. Thanks, too, go to Susan Walters Schmid and Detta Penna for your editorial support and design expertise. Extra thanks go to Neal Maillet for his patience, kinship, and encouragement. Thanks for drawing out the central messages of this book.

One of the ways my publisher improves the quality of the book manuscript it to send it to a team of reviewers. The feedback suggestions I received from Carol Metzker, Roger Peterson, and Sharon Wingron improved the book tremendously. I hope you all can see the changes I folded in based on your good suggestions.

My friends at The Book Designers (BookDesigners.com), who designed the book's cover, always do an exceptional job, quickly delivered.

A special shout-out goes to Nancy Breuer, my writing coach. Thank you, Nancy, for strengthening my voice, and for reminding me that writing is both a gift and a responsibility.

My career has been one of trickery. I am a leadership writer who has led very few people. I write books full of leadership lessons that I've learned from leaders with whom I've worked and then sell the books back to them. My career as a leadership writer, coach, and keynoter stems directly from the lessons that my client leaders have taught me. You have given me more than a gratifying career. You have given me a passionate vocation. Thank you.

I love my family. We are as kooky, playful, loud, contentious, messy, smelly, adventurous, supportive, and loving as a family can get. I wouldn't change a thing. Well, maybe we could look at our phones less. But besides that, I love you all.

INDEX

H

I

J

K

L

ABOUT BILL TREASURER

Bill Treasurer has been designing, developing, and delivering leadership and courage-building programs for three decades. His aim is to help leaders be more confident, courageous, just, and good. He believes leaders should be role models of courage and encouragers of brave and ethical behavior. His ultimate goal is to relegate fear-based leadership to the trash bin of history.

Bill is a pioneer in the area of courage-building and his bestselling book, *Courage Goes to Work*, introduced practical ways to build individual and workplace courage. He also authored *Courageous Leadership*, a comprehensive facilitator training program that equips leaders and training professionals to teach courage-building workshops in their own workplaces. Bill's courage insights and workshops have been taught to thousands of leaders throughout the world.

Bill regularly works with senior executive teams to ensure that they are good role models for the organizations they serve, and to prevent dysfunctional behaviors from causing the workforce to lose confidence in their leadership.

A sought-after keynoter, Bill regularly carries his message of courage to audiences and organizations of all sizes. He is also an active member of the Association for Talent Development (ATD) and serves on the board of ISA—an association of learning providers.

Bill discovered his courage at the top of a one hundred-foot high dive platform as a member of the U.S. High

Diving Team. For seven years he traveled around the world performing in aquatic entertainment productions and has done over 1500 high dives into pools that were only ten feet deep.

Bill attended West Virginia University on a full athletic scholarship and received his master's degree from the University of Wisconsin at Green Bay.

Bill's most fulfilling role is being husband to Shannon and father to his three children, Bina, Alex, and Ian. His family quickly squashes any of Bill's attempts to get full of himself.

Learn more at BillTreasurer.com and GiantLeapConsulting.com. Connect with Bill through social media by visiting Facebook (facebook.com/bill.treasurer), Twitter (@btreasurer), and LinkedIn (LinkedIn.com/in/courage).

ABOUT GIANT LEAP CONSULTING

Founded in 2002, Giant Leap Consulting, Inc., is the world's first courage-building consulting firm. Its mission is to build leadership and workplace courage by driving out fear so that everyone can get superior results. Our services include:

Courageous Future: Strategic planning and futurecasting engagements to set an organization's bold and compelling future.

Courageous Leadership: Comprehensive leadership development and succession-planning programs for emerging and experienced leaders.

Courageous Teaming: Teambuilding programs for executive teams to ensure top team alignment, and team interventions for functional teams throughout the organization.

VR Courage-building: Programs involving geographically dispersed leaders and teams as they participate in a unique and memorable virtual reality courage-building simulation!

Giant Leap takes pride in working with its clients as a trusted partner not a servile "vendor." Its most rewarding work involves working closely with clients to cocreate transformative learning experiences—delivered in-person, online, and through virtual reality—that get real and lasting results. Giant Leap is proud of its client list, which includes NASA, Lenovo, UBS Bank, Saks Fifth Avenue, Walsh Construction, nCino, Hugo Boss, Spanx, Aldridge Electric Incorporated, IES Communications, Total Energies, Southern Company, the National Science Foundation, the Social Security Administration, and the U.S. Department of Veterans Affairs.

To learn more, visit our websites: GiantLeapConsulting.com, CourageBuilding.com, and ManagerialCourage.com. Email us at: info@GiantLeapConsulting.com, or call 800-867-7239.

Berrett–Koehler Publishers

Berrett-Koehler is an independent publisher dedicated to an ambitious mission: *Connecting people and ideas to create a world that works for all.*

Our publications span many formats, including print, digital, audio, and video. We also offer online resources, training, and gatherings. And we will continue expanding our products and services to advance our mission.

We believe that the solutions to the world's problems will come from all of us, working at all levels: in our society, in our organizations, and in our own lives. Our publications and resources offer pathways to creating a more just, equitable, and sustainable society. They help people make their organizations more humane, democratic, diverse, and effective (and we don't think there's any contradiction there). And they guide people in creating positive change in their own lives and aligning their personal practices with their aspirations for a better world.

And we strive to practice what we preach through what we call "The BK Way." At the core of this approach is *stewardship,* a deep sense of responsibility to administer the company for the benefit of all of our stakeholder groups, including authors, customers, employees, investors, service providers, sales partners, and the communities and environment around us. Everything we do is built around stewardship and our other core values of *quality, partnership, inclusion,* and *sustainability.*

This is why Berrett-Koehler is the first book publishing company to be both a B Corporation (a rigorous certification) and a benefit corporation (a for-profit legal status), which together require us to adhere to the highest standards for corporate, social, and environmental performance. And it is why we have instituted many pioneering practices (which you can learn about at www.bkconnection.com), including the Berrett-Koehler Constitution, the Bill of Rights and Responsibilities for BK Authors, and our unique Author Days.

We are grateful to our readers, authors, and other friends who are supporting our mission. We ask you to share with us examples of how BK publications and resources are making a difference in your lives, organizations, and communities at www.bkconnection.com/impact.

Dear reader,

Thank you for picking up this book and welcome to the worldwide BK community! You're joining a special group of people who have come together to create positive change in their lives, organizations, and communities.

What's BK all about?

Our mission is to connect people and ideas to create a world that works for all.

Why? Our communities, organizations, and lives get bogged down by old paradigms of self-interest, exclusion, hierarchy, and privilege. But we believe that can change. That's why we seek the leading experts on these challenges—and share their actionable ideas with you.

A welcome gift

To help you get started, we'd like to offer you a **free copy** of one of our bestselling ebooks:

www.bkconnection.com/welcome

When you claim your **free ebook**, you'll also be subscribed to our blog.

Our freshest insights

Access the best new tools and ideas for leaders at all levels on our blog at ideas.bkconnection.com.

Sincerely,

Your friends at Berrett-Koehler